The 5 Habits of Highly Successful Slackers

[Because 7 is too Many]

K.P. Springfield

AuthorHouse™
1663 Liberty Drive, Suite 200
Bloomington, IN 47403
www.authorhouse.com
Phone: 1-800-839-8640

First published by AuthorHouse 6/05/2007

ISBN: 978-1-4259-6803-8

Cover design by Jenny Petter
Corrupted ideals provided by K.P. Springfield

If you feel compelled to leave feedback about the book, please do so at either
www.slackism.com or e-mail reviews@slackism.com. Good or bad, we'll include
your comments. (Honestly: Like we care how scathing the comments might be.
We have nothing to lose. It is a book about slacking, for God's sake.)

To my hardworking and dedicated wife, the antithesis of anything slacker-oriented.

To my mother, who is proud of her son regardless of how corrupted and misguided his thoughts and motivations are.

To my father, the inspiration for this idea and a closet slacker who hides his true identity like Clark Kent.

To my brother, who couldn't care less about the corporate world and the entire premise of this book.

Table of Contents

Inspiration

One day, while successfully slacking at work, my father called. He asked me how my job was going and I mentioned to him that work had been quite productive, as I had written my first full-length screenplay within a two-month period. After expressing some astonishment, he then asked me where I got the free time to take on such an intensive writing endeavor. "Well, I've got nine hours per day at work," I responded. The astonishment multiplied. If my job was to write screenplays, then there wouldn't be any surprise; however, my job was actually software sales. After explaining to him some of the successful slacking habits I had adopted over the three years at my company, he made a suggestion that I wasn't expecting.

"Son, why don't you write a book on how to slack off at work? That is obviously your forte. I mean, hell, if you wrote an entire screenplay when your job is sales, other people might be interested in hearing how you did it."

What a genius idea my father had. I went to work immediately, at work. I blew off a few things that needed to get done. Okay, more than a few.

A second source of inspiration for *The Five Habits* came when I visited a local bookstore in order to check for similar or related publications on successful slacking. After looking in the self-help and business sections, all that could be found were books on management excellence, leadership effectiveness, executive skills development, how to be an effective communicator, and many other coma-inducing imitations focused on appropriate business acumen.

Virtually every book was the same exact concept packaged in a different cover design with a different author. I thought, "How refreshing would it be to have a completely *antithetical* book on slacking excellence?" It would at least stand out as something remotely original and have a chance of being purchased by a cynical corporate employee – who is far more common than most people think.

However, by far the most significant inspiration came from observing the overwhelming abundance of family and friends who have willingly become overworked corporate drones. I knew it was bad when my friend Nebby bragged to me about how he hadn't taken a vacation in three years, but when I watched my miserable wife trudge to her car every morning to face twelve hours of what she called "hell on Earth," I knew something had to be done.

How demented are we to rationalize that not taking a vacation is a testament to our hard-working demeanor? Why are we willing to put up with "hell on Earth" when there are easier ways to make a buck? The growing popularity of this "burnout nation" concept has been highlighted in publications like *Business Week* and *Scientific American Mind*. It has become a phenomenon – work has taken over the life of Americans, and sadly, many of these people don't love what they do. They just put up with it because it pays the bills and they know nothing different.

Even more depressing is that although Americans take pride in working hard, and always have, with the development of communications technology like e-mail, IM, cell phones, and mobile devices, and the growing inefficiencies of corporate management hierarchy, the American information worker is no more productive than he was ten years ago. In fact, the distractions which these devices create make the modern worker even less productive; especially when not well-trained in how to ignore those digerati devices and complete the task at hand.

I wasn't working seventy-hour weeks when I realized that there had to be another way; it was the blockheaded leadership responsible for our company which made me give up and pursue a life of successful slacking. Seeing those so-called leaders stumble and fumble their way through each agonizing year was a real wake-up call for me as a corporate employee.

They mismanaged teams, pulled immoral employment tactics, lead highly productive people to quit in frustration, and fired those who refused to be "more corporate," which was a suggestion my manager actually made to my face.

The whole concept of Slackism, which *The Five Habits* is based upon, was conceived through poor leadership, excessive bureaucracy, mismanagement, infighting, and underhanded political tactics. Although this behavior advanced their executive images, it came at the expense of hardworking and dedicated employees. *The Five Habits* is partially designed as a wake-up call to those guilty executives and unwitting higher-ups who don't see the turbulence which happens beneath them – for they are the ones who have truly given birth to the advent of Slackism.

With the eventual publication and distribution of *The Five Habits*, my future may include excommunication from corporate society. After much struggle with this potential career-ending scenario (not really), I am sacrificing my corporate future as a successful slacker so that you, the reader, can carry on the torch and live out your profession as a highly successful slacker.

K.P. Springfield
6/10/2006

Laying the Foundation

"What most people want these days is less to do, more time to do it, and more pay for not getting it done."

Slacker. According to Noah Webster, it is defined as *"a person who shirks work or obligation."* What merit is there in writing a book about how to become a successful slacker? I believe that everybody, somewhere deep down inside, has a shred of interest in being a slacker. There are a plethora of corporate sloggers just like me who are not happy with either their career path or employer, and wish they could be doing something better with their lives.

Endless hours are put in day after day at the expense of personal happiness, sanity, and leisure time, simply in order to keep up with "the Joneses." Americans toil too hard to not have wishful moments where we just drop all work responsibility and do what we want, yet *seem* to be productive and diligent. The thought is always in our subconscious, but nobody dares convert these musings into action because it is widely viewed as professional suicide.

As technology becomes ubiquitous, the ability for employees to escape the grips of work grows more impossible. Gone are the days of shutting off your computer and going home to enjoy a healthy work and life balance. WackBerries and cell phones have taken over our being, and because of these menacing tools, management expects a higher amount of productivity out of people. Unfortunately, in order to look dedicated and climb the corporate ladder, most workers oblige management expectations by putting in extra hours in the office while putting off essential stress-relievers such as vacation.

America has got to be the only country where employees brag about how little vacation they have taken in the past three years, as if it were a measure of dedication to their own career. The only measure this kind of pea-brained bragging proves is that Americans are whacked out of their skulls and have become overlabored corporate drones.

However, this type of behavior has not arisen because Americans don't like leisure time and vacation – it is a result of corporations which under-staff teams and put the burden of a three-person job on one individual. Because most Americans are naturally hardworking people, they don't ask questions and attack the monstrosity of work.

Throw in the stifling elements of mergers and acquisitions, bureaucracy, process, excessive management, and the distractions of e-mail, instant messaging, mobile devices, and cell phones, and it is clear to see why Americans are led into the trap of overworking. Although this phenomenon has been happening for years, it seems that the public is finally waking up to the reality that Americans need to stop wasting so much of their valuable life working, especially those who despise what they do. Millions of Americans have been driven into an undesirable career due to expectations set by their family and peers. Eventually, they get into a situation where they make decent money, but are miserable with their career path and can't get out.

The problem is compounded when these same people try to live a lifestyle well beyond their financial means and end up having to work endlessly just to pay the bills. Couples have children, and instead of the mother staying home to care for them, the kids come out of the womb and go straight into daycare. My wife's friend just had her first child, and within a month, she was back to work so she and her husband could continue paying for their house in the Bay Area, their vacation home in Lake Tahoe, and a new $60,000 SUV.

This vicious cycle of living to work perpetuates itself until mental health issues such as insomnia, migraines, depression, and eventual nervous breakdowns take over. Unfortunately, a work-related breakdown happened to a friend of mine, and it took him being in the hospital to realize something in his life had to change. He asked himself, "If I died tomorrow, would I be happy with the life that I lived?" His answer was no. You can't enjoy a hilltop house and a new Carrera if you're dead.

For others, the long hours in the office put a strain on family and personal relationships. Is it any wonder that America leads the charge in divorce rate and hours spent in the office? We have become so possessed with our pitiful careers that the most important people in life – family and loved ones – are left to sit around waiting patiently for our return from a healthy twelve-hour day of work. That hilltop house and new Carrera are also useless if you lose them in a divorce.

In the past year, articles on burnout syndrome and overworking have been featured in publications like *Scientific American Mind*, *Fortune Magazine*, *The Economist*, *Harvard Business Review,* and *Business Week,* proving the phenomenon has become rampant. In fact, the situation has gotten so dire that *Fortune* even released an article about the merits of slacking off at work. Global workforce demands, unnecessary meetings, inefficient management, and unimportant tasks assigned as "urgent" have driven people to the edge of what they can handle in a day's work. The only option remaining is to ignore the requests and slack off. Being a slacker is no longer a defamatory term; the overwhelming work environment of Americans has made slacking a viable solution to reducing stress and establishing a realistic work/life balance.

In addition, several folks in the corporate world have already realized the benefits of successful slacking, and do quite an effective job of it. However, there is no anthem; no official bible of Slackism to reference. I have seen other slacker books and they aren't comprehensive or detailed enough with scenarios and examples. Most discuss taking long walks at lunch, frequent coffee breaks, or making origami to pass the time, but that isn't out-of-the-box slacker thinking; it is elementary, at best.

Some authors talk about how to slack within a culture that has a government mandated thirty-five hour work week where it is virtually impossible to get fired regardless of whether or not you work hard. How difficult could it be to slack in that scenario? There can't possibly be any groundbreaking concepts of successful slacking when management doesn't care what their employees aren't doing. *The Five Habits* takes successful slacking to a whole new level and is designed to advance the game of aspiring slackers within companies that overwork and under-appreciate employees as well as convince the slacker non-believers to convert.

Are You Experienced?

What makes me qualified to write a book on successful slacking? Well, my corporate tenure is probably short compared to many people who might read this prose, but therein lies the beauty. Slackism can be adopted and perfected in a short amount of time with little experience. In three years of successful slacking, I received two grade and pay increases, vacations aplenty, positive annual reviews, and actually managed to get voted into a corporate "Hall of Fame" – all by doing less than three hours of actual work a day.

Wouldn't it be far more intimidating and discouraging if I were to say that this book was written after thirty years of exhaustive slacking research and development? For someone just starting their journey, they may think it will take more than a lifetime to achieve successful slacker status. The art of Slackism can expertly honed in a matter of two years or less, depending on how talented you are at shirking useless responsibility.

I work at a company which strives to produce optimal worker productivity through the software they sell to customers. The company also consistently pats itself on the back for hiring only the most productive talent. Somehow I managed to sneak through the productivity detector, so they should probably put the nix on any further narcissistic congratulations. The irony is blinding – a slackmeister selling software at a company that prides itself in revolutionizing employee productivity. If successful slacking can exist in my environment, then it can exist in a multitude of corporations!

I understand that there are people in this world who love their jobs. Whether it is a corporate gig, their own business, or some other occupation, they cherish waking up in the morning and going to work. For those folks, this book will make no sense and not strike a chord. However, for the remaining vast majority, *The Five Habits* will hopefully be your new anthem.

It may come off as cynical and you may think I am severely demented. You may think I am dishonest and deceitful. You may fret that co-workers share the same sentiments and viewpoints. Worse yet, you might even vigorously nod your head in approval of *The Five Habits*.

The Turbulent Acquisition

I work at a small technology startup which eventually got acquired by a larger company in the ever-trendy practice of corporate mergers and acquisitions. After the takeover, instead of being transferred to the headquarters, my job remained at a satellite campus in our acquisition group, riddled with confusion and lack of organization.

Unfortunately, on top of the satellite campus location and acquisition, our group suffers from massive reorganizations every four months or so, which makes it impossible to let employees settle into an efficient routine which is productive. Within a year, the frustration was so high that our sales team has gone from a core group of dedicated employees to a revolving door of salespeople. This unfortunate company transformation was a significant inspiration for creating *The Five Habits*.

Who knows, maybe if the acquisition wasn't so ill-conceived and lawless, *The Five Habits* wouldn't have been written and in your hands right now. I may have become a content white-collar lackey who came to work every day and did my job to expectations. Regardless, I am proud of who I've become. Being a successful slacker is nothing to be ashamed of, and for all those people out there who don't love what they do, are tired of being overworked and fed up with fighting futility, it is time to get back all that we've lost over the years – the short list starts with money, sanity, and leisure time.

Slackism and The Five Habits Defined

The term Slackism is defined as *the policy or practice of advancing one's available leisure time at the financial and productivity cost of a corporation*. It is based off of the term Careerism, which is defined as *the policy or practice of advancing one's career often at the cost of one's integrity*. As you can see, Careerism is viewed as a detriment to the self for the supposed benefit of an employer. As a counterpoint, Slackism has been conceived as a detriment to the employer for the definitive benefit of the self.

Although Slackism may appear as a completely subversive, dishonest and immoral way to help improve the lives of overworked Americans, executive leaders of corporations have brought the concept of Slackism upon themselves. If it weren't for their irresponsible behavior which has resulted in criminal prosecution, corporate bankruptcy, and the unmanageable amounts of work and stress which lead dedicated employees off the deep end of sanity, Slackism wouldn't even need to exist.

The Five Habits is a comprehensive solution focused around the concept of Slackism and the merits of successful slacking. It is a system designed to advance the perception of a hard-working employee while enhancing leisure time and mental health. Most people associate the word "slacker" with defamatory terms like goldbricker, lazybones or work-shirker, and although these may be accurate moniker parallels, a successful slacker is far different than your vanilla slacker. Successful slackers are perceptive employees who have come to grips with the futility of being productive in a corporate environment, and have decided to do the bare minimum for the enhancement of free time while still appearing productive and dedicated to their employer.

The most successful of successful slackers are able to improve their quality of life, lower their stress levels, work less than three hours a day, and still somehow manage to receive pay raises and promotions. They achieve this monumental feat by adopting five key slacking elements, which are highlighted in The Successful Slacking Sphere (S^3) diagram in Figure 1.

When used properly, *The Five Habits*: Perception is Everything, Whatever!, The Team Player, Procrastination, and Under the Radar work in symbiosis to achieve a harmonious state of successful slacking.

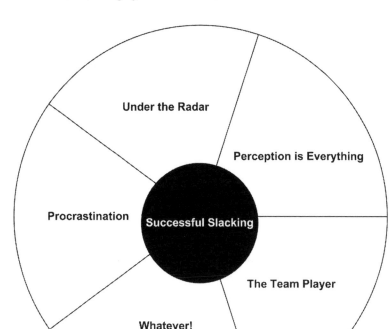

Figure 1: Successful Slacking Sphere (S^3)

Perception is Everything is exactly what the title suggests. In the corporate world, it isn't what you actually do, but what others think you do which makes the difference. By crafting a grandiose perception scheme, you will create the image and aura of a hard-working and dedicated employee while you're actually out kiteboarding. Perception is Everything is the cornerstone of *The Five Habits*. Without it, you will not be able to perfect the other four.

Whatever! is a state of mind which must be adopted in order to avoid the emotional swings which naturally occur when a product launch fails, your bonus is slashed, company stock tanks, or any other blow to the psyche which can affect your mental health and work productivity. By maintaining a Whatever! attitude, nothing can phase the successful slacker, keeping them emotionally immune to the consistent moronic decisions which get made at the executive level.

The Team Player is a role which successful slackers play in order to offset their lack of productivity. Because it is widely proven that managers will put up with people who are less productive so long as they're friendly, easy to manage, well-liked and get along with the team, being a team player is a critical prerequisite for successful slacking.

Procrastination is a tactic successful slackers use in order to test the true importance of tasks and initiatives assigned to them. Because most action items are not urgent, successful slackers use procrastination to buy more leisure time. More often than not, so-called "urgent" action items which go uncompleted seem to disappear, saving the successful slacker a load of unnecessary work. In sales, procrastination can be used as a psychological tactic to bring deals in at the last minute of a quarter; continually proving the successful slacker's role as a clutch salesperson who always closes when it's most critical.

Under the Radar is the state of keeping a low profile so that management and overachievers cannot detect you when sneaking out of the office after a half-day of work. In the spirit of the SR-71 Blackbird aircraft which has stealth-like features to avoid radar detection, the successful slacker adopts similar characteristics to avoid micro-management detection and other unnecessary distractions which can keep one from leaving work early.

Before we delve into the details around these five habits, we will spend a few chapters discussing the traditional slacker profile, why you should become a successful slacker if not already convinced, and perhaps the most important prerequisite to successful slacking – securing the optimal slacker job.

I know the slacker mentality. A 300-page book that drones on and on about useless cock-and-bull does not exist here. It is short, concise, and gets to the crux of how to successfully adopt the slacker habits. If you are an especially successful slacker, at the end of each chapter is a bulleted list entitled "K.P's Notes." If you don't have the time or motivation to read the entire chapter, just turn to K.P's Notes and give yourself a quick slacking **download**.

The Lingo Lexicon

There will also be superfluous references to corporate "lingo." If you are going to walk the walk, you must talk the talk. Therefore, every time **bold** lettering appears, it is referencing a term or phrase that most often heard in the corporate world. Write them down on index cards. Revise them. Memorize them. Put them in a song. If people perceive you to be the corporate guy with the cool lingo, you are fitting right in. It should also be mentioned that as this book was being written, I was at work. So yes, folks, I **eat my own dog food**.

At the back of the book, instead of an index, there is a "lingo lexicon." Each word that is printed in bold can be found with a plain English language definition and explanation, or as close as I can come to plain English (some terms make no sense). There are some universal acronyms common across all companies that are included.

You'll see popular ones like **ROI** and **KPI**, and more importantly, not-so-common acronyms in your specific company which must be adopted. You should already know what S^3 stands for. SAA (Slacker Acronym Adoption) is another critical acronym to learn. SAA can be used to test if a fellow employee is **on the same wavelength** as you when it comes to slacking.

"How is your SAA coming?"

"Oh, it is coming along great," *Wink* "Thanks for asking."

Remember, perception is everything, and if you know even the most obscure of acronyms, well, you are well on your way to slacker nirvana.

Market Research...NOT!

The non-believers might now be thinking, "What kind of research has this kook done to validate these habits?" Are you kidding? Successful slackers don't participate in extensive research unless it is a dire situation. However, slackers somehow find a way to band together like the Mafia. Much like the overachievers club, there is also the under-achievers club.

We share stories and **best practices** to optimize our slacksterity. *The Five Habits* are purely derived from my friends and my personal successes and survival through many job cuts, transitions, and management changes. You will also read about behavior that should be avoided in your quest to become a **best of breed** slacker. Besides, do you really want a bunch of footnotes and research references? Boring! That won't teach you word one about being a successful slacker. Instead of validated data points, we will **peel back the onion** with real-life scenarios and a "lessons learned" section after each habit highlighting a former co-worker who didn't optimally utilize *The Five Habits* to their benefit.

Somebody once told me that 50 percent of all percentages are made up on the spot. Can you believe that? Don't worry. This book won't bore you to death with percentages and pie charts about control groups and other **cradle-to-grave** solutions. *The Five Habits* will hopefully provide you, the aspiring slacker, with useful real life scenarios and **value-added** entertainment.

K.P.'s Notes

- The advent of handheld techno-geek devices have increased the productivity expectations of management, despite the device's inherent ability to distract and keep people from accomplishing any real work.

- Additional elements such as combining three jobs into one, excessive middle management, frequent mergers and acquisitions, and increasing profitability pressures have resulted in endless toil that many Americans put up with.

- Younger workers are often led into undesirable careers due to family and peer expectations. Because the pay can be good, quitting to embark on a more desired path is often difficult – especially for people with exorbitant lifestyles.

- For those who work incessantly with little free time, side effects such as insomnia, migraines, depression, and mental breakdown can take over the body. Others frequently experience strained family relationships and even divorce.

- Articles on burnout syndrome and overworking have been featured recently in *Scientific American Mind*, *Fortune Magazine*, *The Economist*, *Harvard Business Review,* and *Business Week,* proving the phenomenon has become rampant.

- For many, the only remaining option to keep sanity and a healthy work/life balance is to slack off and ignore certain work requests.

- In three years of successful slacking, K.P. has received two grade and pay increases, vacations aplenty, positive annual reviews, and actually managed to get voted into a corporate "Hall of Fame" – all by doing less than three hours of actual work a day.

- The art of Slackism can be expertly honed in a matter of two years or less, depending on how talented one is at shirking useless responsibility.

- Slackism is defined as, *"The policy or practice of advancing one's available leisure time at the financial and productivity cost of a corporation."*

- *The Five Habits* is a comprehensive solution focused around the concept of Slackism and the merits of successful slacking. It is a system designed to advance the perception of a hard-working employee while enhancing leisure time and mental health.

- The Five Habits are: Perception is Everything, Whatever!, The Team Player, Procrastination, and Under the Radar.

- The Lingo Lexicon is the definitive corporate speak glossary found at the back of the book. Every word in **bold** lettering throughout the text indicates a hackneyed corporate term which must be adopted in order to fit within corporate circles.

The Slacker Profile

"Que bonito es no hacer nada, y luego descansar."

– Spanish Proverb

Before we discuss why you should be a slacker, there are a few things you need to understand about the slacker profile. There are certain references, both movie and societal, which highlight the legend of a slacker. Knowing and referencing these pieces of information will immediately get you to the inner circle of the slacker community.

Movie References

The first time my ears ever recognized the word "slacker" was at the age of eight. Therefore, you could conclude my destiny was laid out long before my first corporate endeavor. The term was referenced in one of the greatest movies made in the 1980s, *Back to the Future*.

Another amazing movie made in the 1980s was *Ferris Bueller's Day Off*. This was the tale of a future corporate slacker who had already perfected the art in a high school application. At the critical moment of the movie, where Rooney the school principal caught Ferris playing hooky, Ferris's sister, Jeanie, had the option to watch his future crumble before him or step in and rescue her brother. As angry and resentful as she was at Ferris for continually skipping school, there was a bit of slacker envy present; Jeanie admired his skill as a successful slacker.

I firmly believe she wanted to be like Ferris in some way, so she stepped in and got Ferris out of imminent danger with Rooney. This scenario exists in real life as well. Successful slackers are usually well-liked by their peers. Overachievers and people who play "by the book" may have some animosity against them, but in the end, overachievers admire the successful slacker's **skillset**.

On the topic of student slackers in film, who could forget Jeff Spicoli from *Fast Times at Ridgemont High*? Although not as tactful as Ferris Bueller, Spicoli brought an air of freshness to slacking (or maybe it was an air of cannabis). Either way, it was an approach we can all appreciate as developing slackers. I definitely do not recommend you adopt Spicoli's behavior, because it draws too much attention, but it makes for good conversation at slacker networking conventions where the phrase, "He pulled a Spicoli" is usually heard.

There are two more movies which are widely considered to be the anthem of the common slacker. *American Beauty* and *Office Space* are to the slacker as *Wall Street* and *Boiler Room* are to the stockbroker. Keep in mind, though, that the character behavior portrayed by both Kevin Spacey and Ron Livingston are not **appropriate protocol** for the successful slacker. To blackmail your boss regarding an alleged blowjob, and knocking a cubicle wall down to get a window view while playing Tetris draws excessive attention. Characters like these are the modern-day workplace James Dean rebel: the Clint Eastwood of the corporate space.

Successful vs. Unsuccessful Slackers

There is one common misconception in society regarding slackers that must be cleared up immediately. Many non-believers of our practice feel that all slackers are lazy. The same people who don't do anything at work also go home and become armchair jockeys watching endless reruns and football games. They drive their spouses crazy with incessant lethargy, don't help with household chores, and they definitely don't do anything that involves strenuous physical activities.

This misunderstanding is quite common, as overachievers and other non-slackers fail to recognize the difference between an unsuccessful slacker and a successful slacker. When one is successful in a specific discipline, it breeds further success in other activities. Excellence begets more excellence. Successful slackers work hard at more than just slacking in the workplace. It is especially true when the slacker actually has an interest in a particular pastime.

Ask any successful slacker about their leisure activities (or true interests), and you will be amazed at their accomplishments. You may find that they are reigning champions in their softball league, an Ironman triathlete, an accomplished musician, or even an aspiring writer who has created many published works. Never underestimate the successful slacker. They are far more focused, driven, and disciplined than you think, and refuse to deal with fighting the futility of corporate work environments.

The successful slacker frequently gets confused with the unsuccessful slacker. The unsuccessful slacker is the individual everyone identifies at work as lazy, non-responsive, and unpopular. They are largely reclusive or just have an attitude. They're not personable and aren't well-liked by peers. Just like with Ferris Bueller, you must be able to develop slacker envy. This is done through being a likable and fun person. You have to do people favors and tell jokes. It is quite simple, actually. It is especially simple to be jovial and altruistic when your life is free of stress and responsibility.

Unfortunately, if you are an unsuccessful slacker and reading this book, it will be a long and arduous road. It is hard to switch mentality and behavior once someone is in the unsuccessful camp. Many attempt, but only a few special people make it. Most of the time, a slacker hater has an easier time **transitioning** out of their mindset and joining our team, as compared to the unsuccessful slacker. The reason is because they may hate slackers, but they are good people who work hard in their corporate job. They are likable, but are just too naïve, gullible, or submissive. They drink the **company Kool-Aid** almost as much as their beloved Starbucks.

These people can be saved; we just have to show them the light, which is the goal of *The Five Habits*. It is okay to be a hardworking and dedicated person, but if you are in a workforce culture that is severely dysfunctional and futile, your employer doesn't appreciate or take care of you, and you would rather be doing something else, it is time you consider adopting the philosophy of Slackism.

My Father, the Slacker

Halfway through my creating *The Five Habits,* my father confessed an amazing tale of slacking which I had never heard before. It was at that moment a monumental epiphany struck me – successful slacking may be a genetic predisposition.

Years ago, as a junior executive at a major advertising firm, my father needed a way to get out of working late on a Friday to complete a client project. He had already finished it days before, and wanted to use this advantage to further his hardworking image within the team.

At his company, there was a universally understood symbol that if there was a ball of crumpled paper taped to the office door, it meant one was busy as hell and should not be disturbed. The offices had no windows looking in, so if the door was closed, one could not tell if somebody was actually in the office.

My father had a reel-to-reel tape recorder, and made a ten-second loop of constant typing – *clackety, clackety, clack, clack...* *...ding...clackety, clack, clack, clackety.....ding.* He turned the loop on, put the paper on his door, and left early on Friday afternoon while the rest of the team toiled long into the night.

The artificial sounds of typing rang throughout the office all weekend. On Monday, my father bumped into his manager in the bathroom.

"Boy, you really were hammering away in there, weren't you?" remarked the manager.

"Oh man," replied my father. "Well, you know, I had to get that damn copy done for the client, no matter how long it took!"

"Well, I appreciate all of your hard work."

When he revealed this amazing tale of slacksterity after more than thirty years, it was enlightening — a moment of clarity and self-realization. Thank you for the gift, Father.

K.P.'s Notes

- Successful slackers must adopt a cunning, jovial, and carefree personality (like Ferris Bueller) in order to develop slacker envy with colleagues.
- *Office Space* and *American Beauty* are the slacking equivalent to *Wall Street* and *Boiler Room,* and must be referenced to identify fellow successful slackers.

- There is a common misconception between successful and unsuccessful slackers. Unsuccessful slackers are generally lazy, reclusive, and not liked by peers. They are the traditional slacker which most people are familiar with. Successful slackers are the exact opposite. They're active and popular, and slack only when their efforts are futile and have no worth or benefit.

- Overachievers and slacker haters are easier to convert than unsuccessful slackers because they aren't habitually lazy and inactive.

Why Be a Successful Slacker?

"Each success only buys an admission ticket to a more difficult problem."

- Henry Kissinger

We have defined the profile of a slacker, but there may still be some uncertainty. For some people, this chapter may conclusively determine whether or not the practice of successful slacking will be the right mantra to adopt. Let's get to the point. Why should you be a successful slacker?

The Old Adage

There is a wise saying which states, "Figure out what you love to do, and then figure out a way to make money doing it." Many have solved the first portion of the equation, but the second half continues to elude a distinct majority of people. In addition, activities we love to do usually don't make enough money to sustain lifestyle expenses. Have you ever tried to make a living by being on the Pro Shuffleboard Tour? Try being a professional camper sometime.

My buddy and I started *procampers.com* after our dream to be full-time campers, but we haven't figured out a way to make it pay the mortgage yet (although you don't really need a mortgage as a pro camper).

However, the successful slacker realizes that depending on the opportunity and one's experience, a handsome sum of money can be made working a slacker job which allows them to collect pay for doing leisure activities like pro camping. Therefore, the successful slacker can definitively claim they get paid to do what they love.

For example, I am being compensated a decent amount of money to write this book. Even though I am technically a salesperson, based on how much of my time is spent writing each day, my title should be "author." It is quite annoying that I have other responsibilities like selling in order to keep my job, but at least this slacker job is getting me to the ultimate goal: to be a full-time writer. Therefore, if you wish to get paid for doing a job you love, and you are currently in a less-than-ideal role, the successful slacker ideology should be adopted.

Leisure Activities

Another reason to adopt the successful slacker lifestyle is if you are a hobby fanatic. Because I am a Gemini, it is a serious affliction. There are numerous interests and only so much time in a day. When the work week goes from Monday through Friday, it really cuts in on hobby time. Just for a little perspective, my obsessions include competitive bicycle racing, musical composition, writing, reading, martial arts, tinkering with cars, surfing, skimboarding, skiing, and playing tennis with my wife. How am I supposed to work and get all of my hobbies in? Work simply impedes leisure activities, which is not acceptable. Priorities have to be established.

Fortunately, my wife lets me have freedom to do these activities. We don't have children yet, and for many people, family is the number-one pastime, which is terrific. If your spouse is as understanding as mine, then you have all the more reason to be a successful slacker. It is amazing what you can accomplish in the leisure world once you've perfected the art of Slackism. Before long, most of your hard-working friends will wonder if you even have a job.

Hobbies and free-time activities are mainly why we are alive and happy. Whether your pastimes are raising children, athletics, music, reading and writing, Trekkie conventions, collecting arrowheads, staring at a wall in a dark room all day, or going to dog show competitions, they should be more of a priority in life. We, as Americans, do not nearly spend enough leisure time away from work.

If work makes you happy, then by all means, don't be a slacker. If you like going to work every morning and cannot wait to get there, I and millions of other people envy you. One of the greatest gifts in the world is to be paid money for something you love doing. Most of us struggle for a lifetime to find that kind of situation, but very few get the privilege to live it. If you have found that in your work, there isn't much reason to continue reading this book. I may potentially warp your pure and unencumbered mind.

Misguided Career Path

Regardless of your age, stop and project yourself into the future — to the twilight of your existence. Will you be happy looking back at a long forty years of working in a profession which you may have despised but did because it was good money? Will you be proud of your achievements or regret that you didn't pursue your dream of being a television weatherman?

Will your excessive hours at the office and family neglect turn your kids into juvenile delinquents who appear on the six o'clock news? Will you be proud of bragging to friends that you're the only person you know who has been divorced four times before the age of forty? Are you looking forward to a midlife crisis where you grow a ponytail and pierce your ears in some feeble attempt to regain your youth? These are the kinds of questions you must ask yourself now versus later.

Whether or not one realizes it, we are all in a constant state of transition and change. Even as this book is being written at work, I am making strides toward personal freedom. Working in a corporate environment for all eternity is not my goal – it is merely a means to an end. But in order to get to that end, a lot of pro-level slacking must occur so that I can get this book written!

Don't let work be the excuse as to why you cannot do something you want. If you aren't happy with how things are going, and not happy with your employer, start taking control to make more slack time at work and focus on what you love. If there is one thing a successful slacker never wants to hear, it is when someone says, "Aw man, I would love to go do that with you, but I have to work." Where's the gong mallet? You're gonna get biffed upside the head. The successful slacker never, ever mutters those words. There is always a solution; just convince yourself to figure it out.

Diminishing ROE and "Slacking Shangri-la"

Even if you love work, there still may be a valid argument to become a successful slacker. The concept of diminishing ROE (return on effort) is something that exists within any corporation riddled with bureaucracy, politics, and red tape, whether you like work or not. The fattening of companies with multiple levels of unnecessary management have only exacerbated the concept of Diminishing ROE and "Slacking Shangri-la", which is a terrific development for those who understand and practice the concept.

My wife, a visionary genius, came up with this mind-blowing revelation one afternoon, and it makes quite a strong case as to why successful slacking should be adopted. If there is only one reason why you should successfully slack, this may be it.

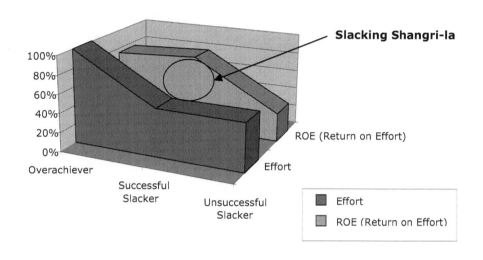

Figure 2: Diminishing ROE and "Slacking Shangri-La"

As you can see from Figure 2, there is a distinct point at which effort does not produce any greater return, and excessive effort (most often by overachievers) actually has a diminishing ROE. The successful slacker always aims for "Slacking Shangri-la," the point at which minimal effort produces maximal ROE. Unsuccessful slackers put in about the same amount of effort as successful slackers, but their lack of practicing the Five Habits prevents them from netting a positive ROE.

Overachievers put in roughly 50 percent more effort than a successful slacker, and usually only get equal or even less ROE than a successful slacker! ROE can vary greatly depending on the level of bureaucracy within a corporation. We haven't done enough research yet to determine the specific statistical significance, and probably never will, so let's just say the more politically befuddled the environment, the bigger your potential "Slacking Shangri-la" can be.

Corporate America

For many, weekdays are spent inside the grips of a major corporation. In the last ten years, with the controversy of companies like Tyco, Enron, WorldCom, Arthur Andersen, and Wal-Mart, white-collar crime and employee exploitation have become rampant. (Whoever came up with the idea to change Andersen Consulting to Accenture is a marketing genius. Can you imagine the negative impact that would have had on the company when the whole Arthur Andersen debacle went down? What foresight. What vision. What luck!) In addition, corporate buffoonery and unqualified leadership have turned many would-be dedicated employees into cynical and guarded individuals who despise their employer.

What about these corporate disasters in the last five years which ruined thousands of people's futures? Was it responsible and dedicated leadership that led those businesses to self-destruct? As a leader, you have the accountability of being a moral and honest individual who makes good decisions for the health of the company and its employees. What happened to those poor folks at Enron was an injustice of epic proportions. I cannot imagine how they must have felt when their entire life savings and equity in the company went whirling down the toilet bowl. Looking back, did those people have the right to slack?

Unfortunately, in today's corporate society, a growing number of companies don't take interest in your personal situation and development. They employ a **churn-and-burn** philosophy, especially in an aggressive industry where growth needs to be blistering and technology is on the **bleeding edge**.

For them, priority number one is **revenue optimization**, not your personal development. If your employer fits this persona, then priority number one for you should be leisure-time optimization. If the company does not take a genuine interest in your development and skills, then why should you put forth a genuine effort?

Alternatively, good companies understand the only way to a turn profit consistently is to take good care of their employees with terrific management, which is refreshing. This concept has been an essential ingredient behind the investment decisions of Warren Buffett in building the Berkshire Hathaway empire. Invest in good management and you will always prosper, because happy employees make for a profitable company. Organizations of this nature are usually the exception rather than the norm.

If your employer doesn't take steps to advance your career, how much of an impact are your individual efforts going to make day to day? If the company is riddled with bureaucracy and politics to the point that it hinders productivity, why try to fight it? Unless you are in some extremely high-profile position, chances are the job will eventually get done regardless of your effort. Why work so hard for a dishonorable employer when you can achieve the same end result by working half as much or less? The successful slacker understands the concept of futility and doesn't bother resisting.

Some unfortunate souls are afraid to slack, in fear of losing their job. They may be the family provider and cannot afford to be unemployed, so they keep their head down and work hard, no matter how bad the environment. On the other hand, some find themselves in a situation where losing their job might be a good thing; however, they still decide to hang around. Why? They've figured out the political game in their organization and don't want to move to a new company where it has to be re-learned. Instead of taking the risk in trying to find a new job, these people choose to take advantage of disjointed **synergies** within a corporation and work them to their advantage; which is exactly what gave birth to the concept of Slackism.

Contrary to what some think, I have a conscience and am not completely anti-establishment. However, I know when someone is trying to dupe me, and you probably do, too. If you feel guilty about putting The Five Habits to work, then you either work at a company that takes really good care of employees, love your work, or love to be manipulated and taken advantage of all the time. If you fall under one of these three categories, then successful slacking probably isn't the right move.

The Five Habits communicates that it is okay to slack if you feel it is justified. There are a lot of people out there who try to take advantage of others. Corporations are no different. In my brief professional tenure, I have seen some cold and unjust actions taken by management against people who definitely did not deserve it. I pity those who do not know better. They are either too naïve or honest and hard working to be a successful slacker, and they get canned anyway.

Unfortunately, hard-working and productive people do get the heave-ho. A lot of it has to do with politics. If a successful slacker gets cut, I don't feel as bad, because at least that person was able to work a stress-free job and coast through the entire event. Plus, if a successful slacker ends up in a **RIF,** it is a far easier gut blow to absorb and forget about. Whatever! At least the person was having fun and getting paid to spend time either doing nothing, pursuing a new career path, or working on leisure activities.

Successful slackers are never found teetering on the edge of a forty-story high rise threatening to jump because they lost their job. Most times, they are the person across the street at the café watching the entire incident (while on the clock, of course).

Societal Pressure and Expectations

Working a corporate job is the default for most people. It is the societal standard after graduating college because Dad said so, or because the career counselor said my skills would be a good match for this job, or because that is what everyone else is doing. The bandwagon effect is probably the most common culprit. Did you take a job at a corporation because you really wanted to work there? Be honest with yourself: How much of it was your personal ambition, and how much of it was societal pressure? I know a lot of people who stepped into the corporate world because it was expected of them. They wanted to build a career as a successful corporate employee; a career.

Careerism vs. Slackism

Career - a field for or pursuit of consecutive progressive achievement especially in public, professional or business life.

Notice that it says "progressive achievement," but only in a professional or business life. All throughout our lives, we are told that "this is good for your career," "this is bad for your career," "you need to be more career-focused," "taking this job will be a step back in your career."

Career is a hackneyed word which is used to help scare people   usually the submissive – into keeping their head down to work hard for the company. It is a euphemism to make the word "job" sound more sophisticated and sexy. People who love their work do not go around telling everyone about their **career advancement;** they lead through example *by just doing it.*

The people who most often gab about their career – which we couldn't care less about – are usually those who live in denial. These unfortunate souls can't come to grips with the fact that they dislike work, so they try to con themselves into thinking the daily fourteen-hour work schedule is "advancing their career," somehow justifying all the time and effort wasted.

In addition, there is positive reinforcement given by superiors to continue down this path and be a good employee. People working in the corporate world for dysfunctional employers don't own their career and cannot steer it where they want to go; management does. They hold career development in front of an employee's face like a piece of marinated steak in front of a drooling German shepherd.

What is even more interesting is the word that follows career in Webster's. *Careerism - the policy or practice of advancing one's career, often at the cost of one's integrity.* Wow! There it is, in black in white inside *Merriam Webster's Collegiate Dictionary.* It says, "… at the cost of one's integrity." Does that unnerve you as much as it does me? The mere definition of the word *career* includes a reference to the reality that it will come at some cost to your personal integrity.

Now that we understand the definition of *career* and *careerism,* let us review what Slackism means. Slackism is defined as *the policy or practice of advancing one's available leisure time at the financial and productivity cost of a corporation.* Being a successful slacker is a statement. We are sending a message: "No more will employees be forced to toil long hours for leadership stifled by dishonesty, bureaucracy, and politics." If the merits of Slackism start a groundswell, we might see a reformation in how corporations behave and treat their employees. Profits can't be made without productive employees, and if nobody is productive, then the corporations who treat employees poorly will start to suffer. In an age of unparalleled worker productivity through the advent of technology, the successful slacker will be the proverbial "wrench in the works" of corporate profitability and **cost efficacy**.

Oh yeah, and if you do adopt Slackism, one of the stipulations is that you can't drink Starbucks coffee anymore (unless someone gives you one of those gift certificate cards. This is the only permissible scenario). I'm sorry, folks, but them's the rules. I'm not some anti-corporate Nazi, but really, the whole Starbucks thing has gotten out of hand, don't you think?

Corporate Victim - Scooter

Scooter was a prime example of how deceitful leadership will fire hard-working and dedicated employees for their own benefit. Scooter was like me – a pre-acquisition employee who lasted nearly three years through the turbulence and change. Of all the people on our team, he was by far the most energetic, happy, team-playing, and outgoing rep we had. He was the MVP of the championship softball team and was a friend to everyone in the group.

The mere fact he made it through the difficult acquisition proved his worthiness as an employee. However, one challenge Scooter continually faced was his anemic Michigan territory. Now some may think that Michigan is fruitful with opportunity, but for our specific technology and targeted customer, it wasn't.

In order to do well in our job, a sales rep had to bring in consistent small deals and occasional larger ones. Scooter had few smaller ones, but would usually do well bringing in mid to larger deals due to the nature of customers in his territory, but they were infrequent. For three years Scooter only hit his number a couple times, but always stayed employed because of his good attitude and commitment to the company.

About a year ago, Scooter, along with a group of other salespeople, were put on **PIP** because of poor sales performance. The action was more a scare tactic than anything, but Scooter complied and did everything management requested of him. After a few months, the PIP issue seemingly disappeared, and Scooter's manager ceased to meet with him to discuss how he will improve his performance to get off of PIP.

Six months ago, Scooter had cold called and uncovered an extremely large opportunity within his territory that was going to be sold in conjunction with a partner. He conducted numerous presentations for executives in the company and negotiated a six-figure contract. At the end of the quarter, he brought it in and sprinted down the hall to clang the sales bell, signifying that the deal was done.

Everyone was ecstatic not only because of the deal size, but because Scooter had finally landed his big fish. It felt good to see him win, because after his three-year struggle to stay employed, he had gotten what was deserved; or so he thought.

After quarter end, company revenue numbers for the quarter were off by over $100,000. The operations team looked into the issue and found that for some reason, Scooter's deal was not booked in time for quarter-end credit. It turned out that somebody in order entry forgot to process Scooter's deal. Scooter was about to go on a planned vacation with his family to celebrate the victory, and would be gone for over a week. He was reassured by his manager, Mr. Congeniality, that the issue would be taken care of, and not to worry.

The deal went off the books and Scooter had lost his big fish. Even though he was told that everything would be okay, Mr. Congeniality did not cover or stand up for Scooter. Because of his historically poor sales performances, Scooter was on Mr. Congeniality's shit list. Mr. Congeniality was an extremely political, image-conscious, and sneaky manager who could never be fully trusted. Scooter was bringing his overachieving sales numbers down, and this botched behemoth of a deal did nothing to help Mr. Congeniality's paycheck.

Because of Mr. Congeniality's disdain for Scooter, the botched deal, and the convenient fact that Scooter was on PIP no longer than six months prior, it all made for a perfect setup scheme to have Scooter fired. The day Scooter returned from his week-plus vacation (he actually came back a few days early to get work done), Mr. Congeniality broke him the bad news. After finding out Scooter had gotten canned, I was flabbergasted. How could he get fired for someone in order entry forgetting to book his deal in time? How in the hell was that his fault?

He did everything in his power to make sure the deal was completed, yet management had no mercy and used the situation to get him ousted. Losing Scooter was a huge blow to my psyche and colleagues alike because he was such a great teammate and personality.

The worst part of Scooter's story was what happened after he got fired, and is a key reason in the argument why you should be a successful slacker if it is justified. Three weeks after Scooter's dismissal, the deal in which he cold called, negotiated, and closed was quietly brought back in by none other than Mr. Congeniality. Do you think he picked up the phone, called Scooter, and told him that a commission check was in the mail?

Mr. Congeniality not only took full revenue credit for the deal, but also publicly downplayed Scooter's efforts in originally working and closing the opportunity. It was one of the most underhanded, dishonorable, and deplorable actions I had ever seen committed in my professional tenure. Scooter was a good man, and did not deserve to be treated the way he was. Anybody who works for an employer that behaves in this manner has every right in the world to make Slackism their mantra.

K.P.'s Notes

- Most people can't make a comfortable living off of doing their hobbies or leisure activities. Therefore, by adopting Slackism at work, successful slackers can definitely say they get paid to do what they love.

- Successful slackers usually have a plethora of hobbies and interests outside of work. While the average American works ten or more hours a day, successful slackers can put their leisure activities at the top of the priority list while doing less than three hours of actual work per day. Unless one loves his or her work, Slackism should be adopted to achieve this state of euphoria and stress-free living.

- Many Americans have embarked on a misguided career path which they despise yet put up with. Many are driven into it though societal pressure from peers and family. By adopting Slackism, one can get paid a salary while refocusing his or her efforts to get their career moving in a more desirable direction.

- The concept of *Diminishing ROE (return on effort) and Slacking Shangri-la* is perhaps one of the most appealing reasons for non-believers to adopt Slackism. Because genuine effort in most corporations is usually is futile and produces low ROE, the concept is perfected when minimal effort produces maximum ROE. Therefore, successful slackers put out less effort than overachievers, yet produce higher ROE and far more leftover time for leisure activities.

- The growing white-collar crime, unqualified leadership, and indifference for employees in Corporate America have spawned disenfranchisement with many perceptive employees. By adopting Slackism, it numbs the blow when executives eventually destroy the company and leave employees with worthless stock and no pensions.

- Careerism is defined as *the policy or practice of advancing one's career often at the cost of one's integrity*. Therefore, Slackism is defined as *the policy or practice of advancing one's available leisure time at the financial and productivity cost of a corporation*.

Finding a Slacker Job

"Be irreplaceable; if you can't be replaced, you can't be promoted."

D on't worry; we're almost to the habits. However, before you can learn and put them to use, you first have to have the right job. If not, you're setting yourself up for guaranteed slacker failure, so take detailed notes.

Lowest Responsibility Possible

There was a memorable scene in *American Beauty* where Lester Burnham decided to apply for a job at a burger joint after blackmailing his corporate boss for a full year's salary and then quitting. When the burger joint manager told Lester that they had no jobs available for management, he replied, "Good. I'm looking for the least possible amount of responsibility." Obviously you don't outright ask for something like that in a corporate interview, but that is essentially the goal in finding the perfect slacker job.

If you are like my wife, a finance manager who reports billions of dollars per quarter in revenues to executive management, it is hard to be a slacker, due to the excessive responsibility – there is no place to hide and build the façade of productivity and dedication. Therefore, in order to be a successful slacker, start with a job that has relatively little responsibility, yet has some kind of importance within the organization. It helps to work within a large company.

If you are in a role that has too much responsibility, apply for a new job right now! Waste no time. The Five Habits cannot be adopted if your job does not allow at least three hours a day to slack. Three hours is a starting point. This book will show you how to double it **across the board**. The most talented individuals may even be able to successfully slack an entire day. Before long, a whole week will go by, and there will be nothing but leisure activities to show for it. However, after adopting The Five Habits, perception to peers and management will be that you had a relatively productive week.

Translating Job Descriptions

The first thing in understanding how to secure a slacker job is reading between the lines in the job description details. Companies always seem to make the job description more intense and serious than the role turns out to be, so don't get worried the first time you read through.

If it says five to seven years' experience, you can get the job with only three to four, especially if the position has been open for a while. When the job description says that the *ideal* candidate will have knowledge of a certain technology or concept; it means you don't have to know word one about any of it.

If the job description has a lot of vague skill sets that include words like "defines," "good communication," "team player," "analyzes," "interfaces," "demonstrates," "listens and positions," "converses in a knowledgeable manner," "achievement oriented," you are on the right path. Because the **bottom line** is each one of these terms equates to one skill – can speak and communicate like a normal human being. You can do that, right?

Also keep in mind that the fewer numerical figures there are in the job description, the more vague and better it is. A successful slacker does not get pinned down by numerical commitments like **performance metrics** and **hard dollar** data. There are some situations where this does occur, particularly in sales. This makes it a little more difficult to slack; however, my job is in sales, and I have been able to slack quite easily.

Always find out how long the job has been open. Do not apply until it has been open for at least a month. The more desperate someone is to fill the job, the better off you are, but be careful. You don't want to fall into a backfill job.

No Backfill Jobs!

If there is one thing the successful slacker does not do, it is apply for a backfill or replacement job, unless you know the person being replaced. What happens here is that if you get the job, you will inherit all of the work and backlog that the previous person left behind. If that person got fired (potentially an unsuccessful slacker), then it could be really bad. You don't want to be responsible for all the wrong or unfinished work of someone else. Not only will you have to work in excess, but you will also run the risk of not being well liked in your group due to constantly being **behind the eight ball**. These two factors combined equal the kiss of death in Slackism.

Look for a recently created position, in a new team, hopefully in a new division of a quickly growing company. It is optimal for slacking because the rules and expectations are not clearly laid out yet. Usually a manager has an idea or a project to **kick off**, but does not have the time to **drive the initiative**. Therefore, they create a new team and hire people to fill it out.

There is a ton of potential ambiguity, change, redirection, and management flip-flops in this scenario, and ambiguity is the successful slacker's greatest ally. The less definitive goals and expectations are, the better your chances of slacking and falsely attaining something tangible. At the end of the day, be able to point the finger at something besides yourself as to why an expectation was not met.

Seek Out Turbulence and Acquisitions

Unfortunately in sales, successful slacking cannot be attained unless you truly are a good salesperson; because in the end, your performance is pretty evident, based on numbers. There are ways to get around this, however. The perfect slacker job is one inside a very turbulent startup or recently acquired company. As was mentioned before, there is an inverse relationship to level of slacking and workforce culture; the more disheveled the culture, the more likely successful slacking will work.

I've been lucky enough to work in a small startup that got acquired by a 50,000-person company. Talk about turbulence – in three years, we have had four different VPs, and I have personally had four different managers. None of the co-workers I had two years ago is on my team any longer. Yes, it has taken a bit of a toll, and the successful slacker has to be adaptive to change, but that is also the key to staying employed. The successful slacker uses the disruption and change excuse to justify why "metrics" and "quota performance" are not **on track**. If you can provide evidence via e-mail or printed documents as to why quota or metrics were not achieved, your future looks bright.

Just like in a court of law, you must prove to management beyond a reasonable doubt why the numbers and goals have not been attained. If your company is organized, turnover is low, and everything is laid out neatly, it will be hard to slack successfully. You, as a slacking protégé, need to find a new job. Think either big, profitable company, or small, profitable startup that may get acquired. Look for disruption and constant change. This is where the successful slacker can thrive.

If your goal is to become an overachiever and climb the ranks of a company, do not hang around if your employer gets acquired. From my experience, employees from an acquisition are identified by the new company and blacklisted from getting any new or better opportunities. Corporations normally do this in much the same way that some stepfathers or stepmothers do not like their newly acquired children. Acquirees, like stepchildren, are often viewed as being excess baggage, and usually treated as such. However, for the successful slacker, this may be the perfect scenario.

Public versus Private

Another critical part of finding a good slacker job is deciding between a public or private company. There are pros and cons for both, but I feel working at a successful private company is a far better deal. At a private company – so long as it is profitable – the pressures of hitting a **revenue target** are far less than a public company. If a public company misses a target, the stock and value of the company will suffer, which brings massive amounts of pressure down on the **powers that be**, which in progression will somehow find its way to you.

If targets are missed at a private company, it isn't nearly as big of a problem. Yeah, the investors will be upset, but the pressure of Wall Street will not come down on management. Therefore, your potential level of stress is far lower. Now, if you work in a public company which is so large and profitable that poor earnings will not directly affect your group, that is the optimal situation.

The company has to be well-established. It has to have significant market share, a lot of cash in the bank, and a product/service that is in demand, so overachieving is easy. It is much easier to successfully slack when you are on a team that overachieves. Remember, there are always overachievers out there. Be on this team, because when it does well, critical eyes look elsewhere. Management looks at unsuccessful teams and makes cuts, especially in sales. As a successful slacker, you can consistently under-perform while the team overperforms, and everyone is perceived as an all-star.

Organizational Logistics

When applying for a new job, make sure there are enough levels of **management buffer** to be optimally sheltered. Any closer than three levels between yourself and a VP, you must reposition yourself. Ideally, your manager reports to a director who reports to a VP. This is enough of a buffer that if played properly, the VP will hardly ever know who you are. It's especially true within a large organization where VPs are usually located in a different part of the country. The more geographically dispersed management is, the more successfully one can slack. If you can do better than three levels, well, maybe I will have you write a foreword in the next edition of this book! Knowing the direct manager you will work for is important as well. Not always will you be so lucky, but even having a friend who may know the manager's personality is a huge advantage. The last thing you want to do is take a job at a company with a brain-donor or a possessed nutcase for a manager.

An example of having a stark raving lunatic manager was when the director of our business unit, Achoo Bleseu, hired a friend to manage eight sales reps. We will refer to him as Kim Jong Il, due to his Korean descent and rigid Communisticesque management style. He got the job purely because of the **buddy system.** Kim Jong Il had absolutely zero qualifications for the position, but still got the job because he used to work with Achoo. Granted, he was an extremely intelligent guy and had engineering degrees from prestigious schools, but he never had a sales management job in his life. He was a technical marketing guy, not to mention the fact he was a slave-driving lunatic.

He lasted only six months before quitting, but in the process, led six of the eight people on his team (who happened to be amazing salespeople) to bail because of his inappropriate behavior and brash management style. He wasted a half-year's salary and cost the company a number of highly productive and successful revenue producers. However admirable that may be, avoid being on a team with a corporate commie like Kim Jong Il. His existence will make it impossible to successfully slack.

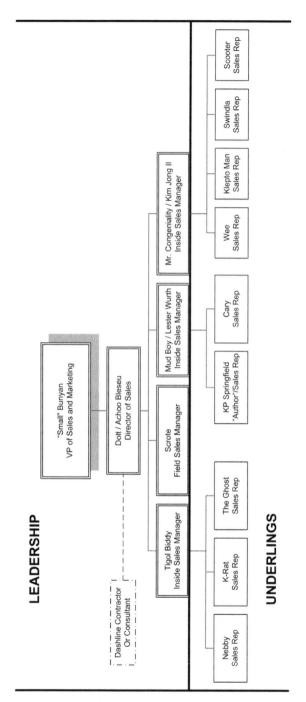

Figure 3: Corporate Org Chart

In order to give you a better idea of how the organizational logistics were within my company, Figure 3 is an org chart of all the zany characters described throughout the book. Anytime you read about a character and are confused about where they fit in, use it as a handy reference.

Achoo Bleseu and the Buddy System – Update!

Late in the creation of The Five Habits, another development occurred in reference to Achoo Bleseu and his buddy system network. Achoo recently announced the hiring of a new director (which makes five in three years) for the inside sales team.

After finding out the news, I did a little research and discovered the new director is coming from the exact same company that Kim Jong Il used to work for; further proving it isn't what you know, but who you know. If Jong's past performance is any indication of the new director, our team will go from barely running on one jet engine to a corkscrew nosedive freefall into the blazing depths of hell.

Slacker Sales Jobs 101

If you are in sales and need a temporary slacker job while looking for a better one, find a company that pays a **non-recoverable draw**. For those not familiar with this term, a company will pay new sales employees their full commission as if they were hitting their quota for the first three months of employment. It is done to help motivate the rep as they are **ramping up** in the new position.

I have seen successful slackers bounce from company to company – especially back during the dot-com era – and collect sizeable commission paychecks for doing absolutely nothing. My co-workers Klepto Man and Nebby, who you will learn about later, did this successfully at a few different dimwitted startups.

There are a lot of good salespeople in the world who start at a company and don't sell squat for months. Management begins to doubt their performance and questions why they hired this monkey dump in the first place. It is a common situation that the successful slacker always avoids. The main reason why good salespeople end up failing is because they did not demand good territory before starting. I don't care if you can sell 3-D glasses to a blind man, you will not be successful if you are trying to sell software in Wyoming, Montana, and *parts* of Colorado. It ain't gonna happen, bub!

The successful sales slacker always makes territory part of the negotiation beforehand. Make sure it is prime territory and get it in writing! If they do not deliver once you start, walk. Your success as a slacker depends on it. There are a lot of great people who could be very successful sales slackers who miss this important element. In sales, territory is everything. Do you want to be cold-calling some five-person horseshoe supply company in Thermopolis, Wyoming, or do you want a **mid-market** software account in Boston calling you?

The sales scenario I have going is corporate Shangri-la. At my company (for tax and legal ramifications), inside sales representatives are paid on an hourly basis, yet they are full-time employees with full benefits. I cannot imagine a better deal (short of being a consultant) for the aspiring slacker. Not only do I get paid hourly and receive overtime any days I work more than eight hours, but I am also getting some great perks. Not to mention the fact that commission gets paid on what revenue I bring in (which is usually not that much). Also, because of my hourly status, I get eighty hours of sick time a year. This is "use-it-or-lose-it" time, so every last hour is consumed by the end of the year. On top of the fifteen days of vacation time and holidays, I am getting about another ten days of sick time. Vacation is extremely valuable to the slacker. It's worth more than money.

The Pinnacle of Slacker Jobs: Consulting

For the more-senior **executives** who have crossed over to the dark side and are reading this book, I have a potentially outstanding slacker job for you. Regardless of background, if you have any expertise in something specific, look into corporate consulting. Consulting has got to be one of the most useless yet prestigious jobs in the corporate world. I still do not understand it. Many have experiences where consultants were brought into a company to make some changes, and underlings often wondered, "What the hell kind of qualifications do these jerks have?"

If you don't have an experience like that, and have seen *Office Space,* then you probably remember the "Bobs," two consultants named Bob who where hired to cut the workforce down and make it more productive. Essentially, that is the role most consultants play in corporations – they come in to do the dirty work because management cannot.

Even though I think corporate consultants provide little **value add**, these folks have it figured out. Here is a job where you are hired by a company to walk in the door, sit around, look at its operations, and then give your opinion on what should be done. Wow! Genius! They pay people for that? If you haven't jumped on this gravy train yet, please, buy a ticket.

In addition, consultants don't have to pay for anything. They usually have the company pay for it. That is why when I follow up on sales leads, I never call consultants. They are cheap. They don't buy anything. They don't have to! As much as I am knocking consultants, it is due to an extreme case of jealousy. Can you believe a successful slacker has slacker envy? It's true! Obviously to be a marketable consultant, you have to have some credentials on an impressive resume. But much like a job description, resumes are complete fabricated bullpucky. Ever wonder why a lot of consultants are full of it? Because most of these people were successful slackers throughout their corporate career and discovered the perfect job.

Consultants are nothing more than former corporate slackers who have gone independent. Why do you think that the Bobs loved Peter Gibbons so much? Because Peter was a slacker just like them, only younger! Is it starting to make sense? There is a lot to be learned from consultants.

Contractor Jobs

Another excellent slacker job is any position that is contract-based. The downside of being a contractor is that you usually don't get amenities like health benefits and 401K, but what you do get far outweighs those silly extraneous items. First, being a contractor means getting paid hourly. When you are an hourly employee, the pay is much higher than someone who is paid on a salary basis. Second, if there is a lot of extra work to be done, a contractor will get paid overtime. Salaried employees don't leave the office until work is done, and they don't get paid anything extra either. If the successful slacker is going to work overtime, God forbid, then he or she better damn well get paid for it!

Companies don't want to pay hourly people overtime if not absolutely necessary, so guess what? You get to work nine to five. Usually you can clock those hours and work even less. Also, as a contractor, there is very little responsibility. Technically, you do report to a manager, but they are far more concerned about direct employees who are salaried. A contractor can blend into the environment like an unused printer in the copy room. If your name shows up on an **org chart** with a dashed line reporting to a manager, you are in the catbird seat.

The goal of a successful slacker is to stay a **dashline** for as long as humanly possible. Dashline employees, whether salaried or on contract, often have very light workloads with little responsibility and accountability. There are plenty of examples which can be referenced, but the most common response people give when seeing a dashline employee is, "Oh, that guy still works here?"

Dashline slackers are usually referenced as "that guy" or "that girl" because people cannot remember their name. As a dashline contractor, you don't have to get to know people all that well, because the contracting company is paying your salary, not the company you are contracting at. If you choose to go down the contractor avenue in the quest to becoming a successful slacker, just be sure to have a good relationship with the contracting company. Therefore, when the contract runs out at one employer, they will call you up to go work at another.

A tactic I have seen other masterminds pull out of their slacker toolbox is either quitting or taking a severance package, working at a different company for about a year, and then returning to the original company as a contractor. This is a checkmate move in the practice of Slackism. The individual left on good terms, went elsewhere, yet kept in touch with the company. Later, the two negotiate a deal for the person to return, but the company wants to limit its risk, so they take the person on as a contractor which is more than okay to the successful slacker. This aforementioned scenario is why you, as a successful slacker, must be the "Team Player." People have to like you so it is easy to return as a contract employee and reap the benefits of ambiguity and low accountability.

Work Attire

Another piece that must be evaluated before taking a job is the work attire. To further prove my optimal work scenario, I get to wear shorts and sandals (yes, sandals) to work every day. A requirement highlighted in my quest for the perfect slacker job was no dress shirt, no dress shoes, and without a doubt, *definitely* no necktie. It serves no purpose beyond cutting off blood circulation to the brain and making one feel uncomfortable. The necktie is nothing more than an expensive silk leash that corporations use to yank and drag employees like a rented donkey.

In most corporations, the tie is a dress code requirement, which is an inconvenience for the successful slacker. What the hell are you supposed to do if you have a noon Frisbee golf date? You can't wear a shirt and tie to that! You have to bring a change of clothes. What a frigging hassle. A lot of people try to convince themselves that ties are a symbol of accomplishment and maturity. I wonder if that is what these poor brainwashed fools think while walking to the office on a scorching hot ninety-five-degree day. Short of a trip to the proctologist, nothing is more uncomfortable than wearing a suit and tie in the middle of August. That is like putting a dog in a car which sits directly in the sun, with the windows cracked less than half an inch. Just say no to the necktie.

Networking in the Slacker Community

Successful slackers tend to band together in a tightly knit group like the Mafia. If you do not know other slackers who work in your community, start reaching out and talk to people. Landing the very best slacker job is no different than landing a top-notch corporate overachiever job: it's about who you know, not what you know.

My buddy Hooptie just secured a potentially superior slacker job at a similar tech company. He found it through talking with a manager who was in his MBA program at school. (I know, I know: You well-trained slackers are probably thinking, If this buddy is such a great slacker, why in the hell is he working AND enrolled in an MBA program? It's a valid question. Hooptie was doing it only because his old employer was paying and would allow a bump in his base salary. Seems to me like too much work for very little gain, but Whatever!)

Hooptie got the job because he became tight with the manager. The job is a new role, in a new team, supporting a new technology that he has never laid eyes on before. In addition, Hooptie has never even touched the company's technology in his life and he has a finance degree. This is a sales support job! Do you see the beauty here? Lots of ambiguity, a support role with poorly defined performance metrics, and a position in which the selected candidate has little relatable experience.

Work Remotely

Another strategy Hooptie enlightened me with was the concept of **working remotely**. Every time we talked on the phone during the week, he was at home. We all know that when one works from home, far less work gets done. It seemed odd because he was in finance at a huge corporation. I figured that his manager must be really lax or not there at all.

Well, it turns out that the manager he directly reported to was based in France. That's right, *France*. This goes back to what I mentioned earlier. Figure out where your manager will be located. If he or she is at another location or even across one of the seven seas, you get a gold star.

Then there are the people who work at home because it is in the job requirements. Most times, they are field sales account managers. Talk about a cush job. These folks usually manage less than a handful of accounts, work from home, and maybe go to a few appointments per week (which most often involve a game of golf, or lunch). It is even better if the job doesn't involve being required to hunt for new customers.

There is one field rep I know who sits on her keister, does nothing, yet collects a monstrous paycheck. Actually, she has so much free time that she's got a side business going. When you call her voicemail, she prompts you to "push one" for her day job or "for my real estate properties, press two." If you have the time to do real estate in addition to your corporate gig, and actually enjoy it, I am jealous – extremely jealous.

Avoid Stress and Anxiety

Have you ever worked past quitting time? For instance, let's say your day is over at three in the afternoon. If you are still there at twenty after, do you ever get this nagging sense of anxiety like you missed the last ferry off an island or you may not make it to you train in time before it leaves? I freak out when it is three thirty and my day should have been over a half hour ago.

Usually the only reason for still being at work is because I am busy hammering away at numerous literary works, which is the only acceptable scenario. However, if it is work-related, the anxiety can eat away at me and cause undue stress. It is scientifically proven that stress has been linked to cancer. Nobody wants cancer, so that is why the perfect slacker job will never keep someone at work past quitting time. Everyone has a rhythm, and it is extremely rude to expect another to break their rhythm just because management has an **action item** which needs immediate attention.

HR Policy – the Recipe for Slacker Success

Successful slacking always requires understanding the HR handbook. It is equivalent to the Bible, and should be referenced wherever possible. Think of HR as the teacher to hide behind when the schoolyard bully is threatening to beat you up. Regardless of what happens between you and management or co-workers, HR is there to mediate and get certain people into trouble. It is especially true within my company, which cannot afford to have any more lawsuits filed against them; they already have too many with their own customers.

As a minority successful slacker, the protections of HR are even greater. The advent of affirmative action and equal opportunity employment has given minorities significant leeway and freedom in the workplace. In addition, if you are a disabled veteran or have been in the service, it would behoove you to understand the details of company HR policy surrounding your particular rights.

I have seen the race card played occasionally, and it works every time. Most recently, there was a woman who did not get along with our manager, Lester Wurth (who you'll learn about later on). She parlayed a legitimate medical condition along with her complaint to HR about Lester in order to get permission to work from home three days per week, and her job was inside sales. (In case you aren't familiar with inside sales, nobody works from home!) Before long, I started asking questions as to where she was. Because of her medical condition, her complaint to HR, *and* the fact she was a minority, she had the hat trick going. She was untouchable.

For jury duty situations, some companies will pay for the entire tenure should you ever be called to serve. Jury duty does suck canal water, but it is still better than being at work. Plus, you can usually get out of it early and tell Mister Manager that you have one more day to report, so long as you have the paperwork to prove it.

Also look into HR policy regarding sick days. There is a term which some companies refer to as "sick events" which is one continuous, horribly bad string of sickness. Some corporate policies regard a sick event as only one day of sickness. That means you could be out an entire week and only get docked one sick day. Obviously, if there are a certain number of sick days allotted in a year, the successful slacker uses those days up first. It is not acceptable to have leftover sick days at the end of the year.

Not only does understanding HR policy protect slackers in a defensive sense, but it can also be used in an offensive way. If you are at odds with a direct manager or co-worker for whatever reason – whether personal or not – and they act in violation of HR policy, use it as a blackmail device. At work, asinine behavior abounds. Most people have no clue their actions are a grave violation of HR policy.

By pointing out their folly, you get the upper hand and the leeway to slack even more. Obviously, you must approach this with extreme caution and only use it in a last-case scenario, but it is there in a pinch.

Missouri – the Slacker State

For those thinking about not only changing jobs, but maybe also moving to a new part of the country to get a fresh start, look into Missouri. According to a recent online poll done by American Online and *Salary.com,* The Show-Me State is number one at "wasting time" when it comes to working on the job. Apparently, three hours and twelve minutes per day is what the average worker in Missouri wastes, as opposed to the national average of two hours (not including lunch breaks). Now mind you, this is an average.

What I want to know is who are those jerks keeping the average so low? I am slacking at least six hours a day. It isn't encouraging to see people slacking on slacking. At least Missouri has the average above three hours, which means that there are probably a fair number of people at or around the six-hour mark. After adding in about an hour for lunch, that leaves about one hour per day of solid work because successful slackers dare not work more than eight hours.

The best part of this survey was when they broke down what people are actually doing instead of work. Forty-four percent of all respondents said that they waste time with personal Internet use. Activities such as reading e-mail, instant messaging, playing online games, and get this, responding to online *polls! Touché!* AOL and *Salary.com* were only adding to the lack of productivity within the workplace, which is commendable.

I think we can attribute the relatively low slack hours per day in the poll results to the fact that successful slackers are too busy with leisure activities. They don't spend free time filling out online polls about how much they slack. You might as well be working if you are filling out online polls about slacking. That is not what a successful slacker considers fun. Plus, by doing this poll, there is actual documentation certifying the practice of Slackism, which is like writing your own confession of guilt. Successful slackers never incriminate themselves.

K.P.'s Notes

- Seek out a job with the lowest possible amount of responsibility while still retaining some kind of importance to the company. These types of jobs are most commonly found in larger corporations.
- Read between the lines with job descriptions, as they always sound more intimidating than they actually turn out to be. Look for job descriptions which contain words such as *the ideal candidate, good communication, analyzes, interfaces,*

demonstrates, defines, listens, and *team player.* Because all of these equate to one skill: the ability to speak and communicate like a normal human being.

- Unless you know the person who worked the job before you, do not take a backfill job. The person leaving may have gotten fired and will leave a mountain of unfinished work, putting you in a precarious situation doomed for failure.

- Seek out a new position in a new division of a growing company. The ambiguity and lack of defined processes will leave plenty of room for successful slacking.

- Despite its downtrodden environment, seek out recent acquisitions and turbulent workplaces so you can point the finger of low productivity elsewhere.

- Large private companies are a better shelter for successful slacking due to the lack of performance pressure from Wall Street and shareholders.

- Position yourself at least three levels below a VP in order to maintain low visibility and avoid unnecessary pressure from executives.

- In sales, always demand territory in writing before accepting a job. Successful slacking in sales cannot exist without having a territory filled with easy deals.

- For the more experienced, consider going into consulting, which is the pinnacle of successful slacking. Many consultants are former corporate slackers who have discovered the gravy train and low responsibility of going independent.

- Contract jobs are another lucrative option filled with high hourly pay and low responsibility. Because most managers are busy micro-managing their salaried employees, contractors are left alone to collect far more money and leisure time.

- Understand the work attire rules. Any company which requires a suit and tie is not a viable option for successful slacking. Changing clothes in order to attend a three-hour midday Frisbee golf game is unacceptable.

- Jobs which enable people to work remotely equate to one thing – effective successful slacking. The further away your direct manager is located, the better.

- If you are a minority or have a health condition, understand and use the HR policy to protect you from management scrutiny like a teacher from the schoolyard bully.

Habit One: Perception Is Everything

"Don't just do something, stand there!"

If it looks like dung, and stinks like dung, it is most likely dung. Note that I said *most likely*. Perception is everything in the corporate world. If you look like a hard worker and act like a hard worker, it is most likely you are a hard worker. In the absence of tangible results, the successful slacker relies heavily on using perception to build pseudo-success. That is one of the main observations made in my brief tenure as a corporate employee and why "Perception Is Everything" is the first and most important of The Five Habits to understand.

Politics

It is amazing what can be accomplished if the mirage of a dedicated corporate employee is well-structured. There are lots of moving parts in building a really solid foundation of perception. At the center is the ever-present game of corporate politics. Unfortunately, if you really want to perfect the art of successful slacking, a good understanding of company politics is a **key** objective. You do not have to be the grandmaster politico guy, but it will really help to understand who holds the influence in the organization.

Title means less than influence. Just because someone is a director or a VP does not automatically make them influential. I have seen some real dunderheads in high-level positions. They had about as much impact as a shopping cart careening into a brick wall. Lower-level managers with some major political game can easily set their direct boss up for certain death. In one instance, a manager by the name of Tigol Biddy single-handedly ousted another woman who was the director of the business unit. This was after the director demoted Tigol Biddy in the hopes she would quit. Well that didn't happen.

Payback is a bitch as they say, and because Tigol Biddy understood the business way better than the director did (remember, dunderheads do get high-level jobs), she was asked to a large executive leadership meeting. After positioning the director as incompetent in a politically savvy way, within two weeks, the director packed up her belongings and got redeployed to wreak havoc in a different business unit. The successful slacker identifies this political superiority and automatically befriends a person like Tigol Biddy. If you succeed in getting tight with this person, they will **go to bat** for you in all situations.

I can remember a few times where my performance was sub-par (one time due to my ineffective slacking, and another time out of my control), and **the leadership team** was having discussions about possibly **letting me go**. Tigol Biddy went to bat and was convincing enough to keep me employed. If a dunderhead had represented me, the leadership team would not have listened to the argument, and I would have been escorted out by security.

Be selective in choosing an upper-level voice, because if you choose the inferior influencer, it will be more difficult to slack successfully. Therefore, the scouting process has to be long and thorough. It will probably take at least three months or so before you can make an educated decision on who will be the best prospect. It is a crucial step in building up perception, so be diligent.

Once the proper manager, director, or even a VP (if that is the case, you are my superior in Slackism) is selected, the foundation is laid. Now go for visibility, but only to those influential people who you've befriended. Do not become close with too many political masters. Stick with the one who you think is the best. Worst-case scenario, if the person gets fired, and you are well-liked, you'll get a job with them at a new company.

Peer Groups

Identify who the biggest overachievers are in your group of peers. Make sure that you are either on their team or know them personally. Hang and be seen with them – it doesn't matter whether you like them or not. As soon as the work day is over (which is usually far earlier for you than for the overachiever), you don't have to call or talk to them. They're going places, and by gum, you are too! Well, at least that is what people think.

Be careful in this situation because an overachiever is often highly intelligent. Sometimes they are gullible and overachieve because they like to be ruled by fear, but on average, they are sharp. If you are not completely honed in the successful slacking department, they will pick up a scent of slacking. If this happens, they will distance themselves, or worse than that, blow your cover as a slacker to upper management, which is a huge setback. Approach the overachiever with caution as you would a poisonous snake. They do not want you to get credit for all their hard work.

Just as cautious and selective the process should be in finding an influential manager and overachiever; the same is true in selecting who not to be seen with. Every company has the disgruntled employee group or the unsuccessful slacker clan.

There may be some interesting characters and personalities you identify within either clique, but resist the temptation to be seen with them; it will ruin your perception. Go ahead and call or hang with them after work, but don't eat lunch at the café with them every day.

A specific example came from my co-worker known as "The Ghost" because he was virtually invisible at the office and personified the fifth habit "Under the Radar." The manager I mentioned earlier, Tigol Biddy, had a conversation with him about how he was being viewed as a grouchy employee due to his association with a few folks in the disgruntled **legacy** brotherhood. Even though he was very quiet and a hard worker (at least that's what you think), his image was being tarnished because of who he was hanging out with.

Tigol followed up with an e-mail to The Ghost about his conduct. She was excellent at the game of **CYA,** and her favorite thing to do besides bore people to death with her horse riding analogics was to send out e-mails with unbounded words inside quotations. The e-mail would read something like:

Dear 'The Ghost,'

In follow up to our 'one on one' today, I really want you to adopt a 'refuse to lose' attitude so that we can continue our 'pitch to switch' campaign and win customers. In

order to do this, we need to have our 'ducks in a row', so
please make the necessary efforts to 'refocus' and be 'in it
to win it'.

'THANKS!'

Tigol

Tigol Biddy, the superlative politician, made sure that The Ghost realized his folly – and if The Ghost ever quit or scrutiny was placed on Tigol Biddy, she had documentation to prove he was a **management problem**. Unfortunately for The Ghost, he still suffers from negative perception through fraternizing with **bad apples**, and once in the pit, it is very hard to climb out.

Identify Overachieving Partners

If you work in a sales organization where it is encouraged to team with partners, do everything possible to take advantage of the situation. Employ the same process described above to find overachievers with the partner channel. You will quickly find that by teaming up, your sales numbers will skyrocket, and you'll be spending far more time with Arturo drinking *cervezas* down at the boat dock.

Executive leadership from both the partner organization and your company will praise your efforts of teamwork and selflessness. Depending on the company, you may not get list-price credit by letting the partner bill your customer, but who cares! Would you rather get paid 100 percent of list price and do 100 percent of the work, or get paid 75 percent of list price and do little to zero work?

I was recently introduced to a sales rep at a partner company who brought me in on a rather sizeable deal. This guy gave me a background on his experience, and when he said he did over 300 percent of his number the last few quarters, I started doing the gold digger dance. Not only will this guy help me hit my number, but I will also achieve it by coming into the office four days a week and working on this book each of those days. It can be exhilarating to have a partner who is so successful, but just like the overachiever in your direct team, the partner may get a whiff of slacking if you do not give him something back.

If you have any prospects, bring the partner in on your deals so that there is no animosity or suspicion that you aren't giving back to the relationship. In my situation, I am throwing this guy most of my deals. I am completely okay with not getting full list credit because of billing through the partner. I figure that by passing him deals, he will work harder and close more than I would going direct. So far, it has been quite a successful venture. Arturo at the boat dock also appreciates all the extra time I am spending there drinking Dos Equis with him.

Shameless Self-Promotion

Now it's time to make wins known to everyone. Whether it is acquiring a new customer for big money, completing an important project ahead of schedule, or successfully urinating with no hands, make sure the entire organization knows about it. How do you achieve this without being overtly annoying or braggadocios? If it is a sales scenario, and you've won a big deal, ask the customer if he or she was satisfied with the experience. If they say yes and you have a good relationship (most successful slackers do), then have them write an e-mail of satisfaction to you and your direct manager and pass it up the **chain of command**.

Have the customer write accolades like "above and beyond expectations," "was patient and extremely understanding," "took the time to listen and cater to our needs." This kind of stuff is worth more than you think with management. When they see you are superior with handling customers, expectations in other areas such as call volume and revenue are far lower.

If you work at a company like mine where there are superfluous budgets to make internal videos and other unnecessary marketing material for the group, get involved. For instance, a co-worker of mine (who is an uber-overachiever) closed a large deal with a new customer. The marketing team did a case study on the customer, and the sales rep was involved in the video that was produced. He was filmed using the technology to communicate with co-workers. One of the technologies was instant messaging, so what did he do? He used my name in the video as the person he was messaging with.

In addition, he showed an e-mail I sent him and the subject which says "lead for you." Executive leadership watches that case study, sees my name with a reference to a lead, and subliminally thinks I am productive. Now I must admit that sending the lead to my friend was strictly coincidental. I was just doing a personal favor (as most successful slackers do), but it paid off with far more benefit than originally anticipated.

In our group, there is the "Hall of Fame" for sales reps who win a certain amount of customers by switching them from a competitive solution. Only about ten reps have achieved this stature, and once in, you get your picture on the wall in the hallway for everyone to see for all eternity. Talk about the perfect image booster and self-promotion tool — man, this is the zenith! By complete surprise, somehow my mug shot made it up on the board. It may have been because every single deal I ever closed was reported as a competitive win, whether it was or not. Eventually, all those modest deals got me in the annals of corporate history. Having "Hall of Fame" on your résumé is like having an all-access VIP pass at a rock concert. You enter the interview, flash your résumé and say "HOF, baby. When do I start?"

"Excuse me?" says the interviewer.

"HOF, man. I'm in the hall. How much is my signing bonus?"

"You haven't even interviewed yet."

"Look, bro, do you want a HOFer on your team or not?"

"Well, okay," he responds. "Can you start tomorrow?"

"Tomorrow?! Hell no. Two weeks. I'm going on vacation first."

"That should be fine," says the interviewer.

"You damn right it's fine. **IYF!** HOF, baby!"

If a successful slacker makes it onto the "Hall of Fame" board, it is like being elected to the supreme court. Unless you decide to quit, you are there for life. Nobody is going to fire an employee in the "Hall of Fame." If they do, you can sue them and win. Just tell the judge that they retired your keyboard.

The Myth of Quota

I am sure there are some people reading this and scoffing right now. "No way" they say. "It is cut and dry, if you aren't selling, you aren't producing." Baloney! Trust me. Out of the thirteen quarters at my company, I have hit quota about three times, if that. Therefore, with some quick **back-of-the-envelope math**, that comes to hitting quota only 23 percent of my entire tenure. But somehow, out of the thirty-five salespeople who started with me three years ago, I am one of only about eight salespeople left. How did I do it without hitting my number? I came somewhat close.

I would usually hit between 70 and 85 percent of the number. In a really bad quarter, I may come in at about 50 percent. There is a lot of room to slack successfully when you are only hitting 75 percent. However, please keep in mind that I found the right slacker sales job. It was a startup acquisition that was made by a 50,000-employee company. There has been a lot of turbulence and unrest.

Not only do I have e-mails from customers saying how good I am, but I can also point the finger at a myriad of problems which prevented me from hitting the number. See how perception can work? It is easily good for making up a 30 percent gap in quota attainment.

Ambiguous Goals and Commitments

Another key to building positive perception is setting very ambiguous goals and **commitments** in annual review meetings. There is that word again: ambiguous. Ambiguity is the successful slacker's greatest ally. If management cannot pin you down to something specific, there is no accountability. Therefore, the parameters set have to be easy to achieve. "Commitment" is the term that my company recently used to replace the word "goal." I guess goal did not have as much accountability weight in it.

In light of this, it is even more important now to make my commitments as vague as possible. Actually, my annual review is supposed to be done by tomorrow, and instead, I am writing The Five Habits. Slackism is a beautiful thing. Be vague with goals and commitments. If management tries to push and put more accountability into goals, just say you will put forth the best effort possible, but "There are **interdependencies** with other team members which may potentially hinder commitments."

That will automatically open the door to ambiguity and gives you the ability to point the finger at someone else if commitments are not met. A successful slacker must know his limits. Do not go beyond them, or you will be spending way more time at the office than previously anticipated.

Numbers are a successful slacker's worst enemy because of their inherent exactitude and lack of blurriness. My buddy who is in finance once told me that if someone asked him for a figure, he'd give it to them but further mention that it is a **high-level number**. This is corporate lingo for "guess a number between one and a million."

However, because he included that disclaimer, he was not accountable for validating it. If there is exactitude, there is no room for fudgery. That is why I was so good at English. With words, everything is open for analysis. One can paint a far better picture of ambiguity with words than numbers. Unless you can confidently back the numbers up, well, avoid them as you would a mullet-head in a 1988 Camaro IROC.

Artificial Performance Metrics

Employees in call-centers all over America – especially inside sales and customer support – are held to **KPI**s: parameters such as calls per day, hours of **talk time**, activities in the **CRM** tool, and number of demos or presentations in a week. There are numerous ways the successful slacker overcomes the obstacle of fulfilling daily requirements. As was mentioned in the chapter about finding a slacker job, the ideal company must be turbulent or in a state where systems are all discombobulated. If this is the case, then fudging phone calls and demos is not a problem. Here is the strategy.

When you first start calling or prospecting in a region, make note of all the companies that have automated voice answering. Write these phone numbers down. Be sure they are in or near your territory. Even though my company is pretty disorganized, it is easy to run a phone report and see what area code is being dialed. I have actually seen some boneheaded unsuccessful slackers dialing phone numbers in California (where they live) when their territory is on the East Coast! The successful slacker knows better and makes calls in their own territory with a list at least thirty numbers long. Do not dial the same phone numbers on the list in the same order. That behavior will blow your cover and management will confront you.

Mix the numbers up. Go top to bottom, then bottom to top, then middle, etc.

Talk time can be a little more difficult. In this scenario, you actually have to be on the phone for a period of time talking to somebody (or so management thinks). Once I stumbled upon a talk time gold mine. I dialed our customer support hotline (a 1-800 number, which is acceptable), and when the automated voice said "goodbye" after I had not selected any options, guess what? The phone number never hung up on me. The voice stopped, but the line was still connected! "Eureka!" said the successful slacker. I call this number at least four times a week for an hour of quality talk time. It's been going on for two years and management has never said a thing.

However, on one occasion, my boss, Lester Wurth, did walk into my office and asked "Hey, are you on the phone?" after seeing I was connected.

"No, what's up?" I totally forgot I was still on the line. He looked at my phone and seemed confused.
"Your phone line is still connected," he said.

"Huh, that's strange! They never hung up!" and I quickly hung up the phone.

"Weird," Les responded.

"Yeah, really weird."

It was a close call and an uncomfortable moment. The worst part of this story is that it has actually happened on three separate occasions! Hey, even the best of us make mistakes. However, if he tried to bust me, I'd just say that I was on the phone with our tech support. It was a very lucky find that still works to this day. The perception is that all my metrics are met, when in actuality, I am writing this book!

Looking back, I should have pulled the "I'm on the phone but not really" move on Les. That occurs when someone you don't want to speak with appears at the door or cube, and looks in to see if you are on the phone. When they do this, give them the universal "one minute" point, or point to the phone and start cryptically talking with someone. This skill takes some practice. It isn't very easy to have an artificial phone conversation with an automated attendant or dial tone. It happened to me just this morning when my director, Achoo Bleseu, knocked on my door. He hadn't said a word to me in over a month, and I liked it that way. He looked in my window, I pointed at the phone, and the talking magically happened.

"Uh, yes, that's correct Seymour. The demo is scheduled for 9:30 tomorrow," I said.

"If you'd like to make a call," replied the automated attendant. "Please hang up and try again. If you need help, press star now."

Achoo nodded, saw me in the middle of negotiating a demo, gave a thumbs-up, and walked away. I successfully avoided an entire conversation with him by faking a phone call. As a bonus, Achoo perceives me as a true phone monkey who is "in it to win it" with my **"game on."**

As much as I enjoy dialing numbers and hanging up after a minute or so, sometimes I wonder if it is more work to actually dial a company number, navigate through their name directory system, and hit random buttons rather than actually talking with a person. Regardless, I have uncovered some rather entertaining names from the phone directory system such as Greg Doody, Karina Dooder, and Ravisharma Balaswamarathimarzipan. It is hard work dialing forty fake numbers every day. Try it sometime. It is also quite challenging to surf the Web and hunt through a phone directory simultaneously, which is the successful slacker's interpretation of **multitasking**.

A co-worker of mine once mentioned that at his old company (which was a chief competitor) they were so paranoid and obsessive that management would actually track the demos one did by the IP number (Internet address where a connection is coming from). Therefore, if you log a completed demo in the CRM, they cross-referenced the demo tool to see if you were actually logged in. Not only that, but they also checked to see how many others were logged in and what their IP addresses were. This is not the ideal company to be working at if you want to successfully slack. I am sure a really good slacker could figure out a way around this, but damn, if you can't, well, remember the mullet-head in the Camaro IROC? Yeah.

Résumé Perception

If you are a successful slacker and are applying for a new job internally or looking outside the company, start building up that résumé so people perceive you as an all-star hot prospect. Like I had mentioned earlier, job descriptions and résumé are at least 70 percent bullpucky. The remaining 30 percent is heavily twisted truth. I know this because I also used to be a recruiter.

This section is not meant to be a "how to" on fudging a résumé, but maybe something which is covered in a future volume if these couple ideas **strike a chord** with a broad audience. Just like in a job description, include vague words like "mentored." *Mentor* is a great word because it means you have leadership experience without formal recognition. If you say you were a manager and the employer checks your job history, you will be called on it if you weren't. As a "mentor," though, it is open for opinion. My manager might not consider it mentoring, but I sure do! Ambiguity, there it is again.

If you did some formal training on a technology or a process, include that in your achievements as being "officially certified." It sounds really good even though it means virtually nothing. Because if you are a successful slacker, the training received probably went in one ear and out the other, or better yet, you weren't even there in the first place!

Lessons to Be Learned from Klepto Man

Numerous lessons in perception can be learned from the successful slacker, however, there are more which can be acquired though aspiring slackers who aren't quite there yet. A colleague of mine, let's call him Klepto Man, is in this camp. How can we identify him as such? Well, there are several behavioral characteristics which tarnish his perception. Although he tries really hard, Klepto Man has not established perception of his productivity. He has been busted for the repeated phone calls to his home area code to have hour-long conversations with his wife. He has also been heard calling different companies, then quickly saying, "Oh, I'm sorry, I must have dialed the wrong number," then hanging up.

Worse than all of that, he has built a reputation as being a guy who loves tits and ass. Don't misunderstand; I love T&A as much as the next straight man, but the successful slacker does not make it known at work... ever! Klepto Man will take a two-hour lunch, have some beers, and go get a five dollar "strip" steak at the local titty bar. After a while, word gets around. You do not want to be the "strip" steak guy.

If that isn't enough, Klepto Man would sit all day and surf the Web, looking at porn. In addition, he would get on personal sites and pick up chicks with his Webcam. Just yesterday, my co-worker Nebby caught Klepto Man pulling his shirt up for a girl with the Webcam. Surf for porn and do virtual strip shows all you want when you get home, but don't dare do it at work! Your perception and image will be compromised.

Another sad fact about Klepto Man is he believes he's pulling a fast one on everybody. He actually thinks he is successfully slacking, but in reality, everyone knows Klepto Man's game. He is the type of guy anyone with half a brain can see right through. I pity him, really; especially when Klepto Man runs around the office all day claiming booty like Blackbeard the pirate.

When someone either quit or got fired (which happened at least once every two weeks), before the person even hit the pavement, this grubby devil went into their old office and took things like their flat-screen monitor, television (yes, we had TVs), wireless gadgets, Webcams (for multiple-angle strip shows), and anything else he could get his hands on. Walking into his office was like walking into a Chinatown thrift store, packed to the ceiling with junk. What he could not use, he usually took home to his family, consisting of five children.

One morning, I went to the break room to get some coffee. The pot was empty, so I made more and went to the bathroom while it was running. I left this really nice coffee mug on the counter. I came back two minutes later, and the mug was gone. Lo and behold, Klepto Man was standing nearby, hiding the mug.

"Hey, how's it going, man," I said. "Is that my mug?"

"Oh! Uh, yeah. I knew it was yours, I was just hiding it from you," he chuckled.

Now, how the hell did Klepto Man know it was mine? He's never seen it before, and he didn't see me enter or leave the break room. Klepto Man was plotting to steal my coffee mug! If you want to be a successful slacker, hooking your colleagues' items is not a great way to achieve your goal.

He did a similar thing with food. If we had a catered event, he would pile up his plate, eat, and then hang around like a vulture waiting for an animal to die. As soon as everyone was done eating, he would start to pack up the food (usually without asking first), and take it home. He even collected aluminum soft-drink cans and piled them up on his desk so that when he accumulated enough, he could go recycle them for a few measly dollars. It was a sight to behold.

This behavior in and of itself is not a bad thing. I don't hold it against people if money is tight and they do what they can to make ends meet, but honestly, this guy made decent money and had great benefits. Also, the "strip" steak and Blackbeard behavior didn't help the situation. His perception was already tarnished, and anything else that he did just made things worse.

Klepto Man had also gotten other people into trouble with his stealing of company property. Recently, Klepto Man went in to the office of my buddy K-Rat after he quit the day before. Klepto Man notified Nebby that there was a wireless headset in K-Rat's old office, and that if he wanted it, he should grab it. Nebby never took items out of other offices, but for whatever reason, he listened to Klepto Man and took the headset.

The following day, our group admin sent out an e-mail asking who had taken K-Rat's phone headset and other random items. Nebby couldn't believe it and confessed immediately. The admin got extremely angry with Nebby, and his image suffered because he heeded the advice of Klepto Man. Nebby had never taken anything up to that point, and since Klepto Man had historically confiscated so much property without getting in trouble, Nebby thought it would be okay just to take one item that he really needed to use. Don't let a guy like Klepto Man ruin your image.

Klepto Man used to work on the same team as the infamous manager Kim Jong Il. Klepto Man kissed his ass quite a bit because he knew that Jong was a lunatic and hated all of his direct reports because he thought they were inferior. Klepto Man was trying to get on Jong's good side. A co-worker of Klepto Man was working a sixty-thousand-dollar opportunity and had repeatedly told Jong that it would be closing within the month. She suddenly quit, and after Klepto Man raided her old office for any good loot, he told Jong that they were both working the opportunity and that it was close to closing. Klepto Man wanted to continue working the deal so he could get full credit. Jong was not convinced, knowing that Klepto Man was a con artist of massive proportions. Klepto Man insisted that he had been on multiple calls with the customer. Jong **took the initiative** to call the customer and find out the truth.

The customer told Jong that he had never spoken with Klepto Man. Jong then asked if the opportunity was still set to close by month end. The customer was taken aback and replied that they weren't planning to make a decision for another three months. The opportunity was used to simply buy time before quitting, but even better, Jong caught Klepto Man in one of his numerous lies.

"Hey, Klepto Man," Jong said. "I talked with Veracity Corporation and they mentioned that they've never heard of your name, and that the deal is nowhere close to closing."

"Oh, yeah, well, uh, you see…"

Klepto Man was busted. Even better, Klepto Man kept lying to cover up his lie, thinking that Jong would somehow believe him. It did nothing for his positive perception and killed all the ass-kissing efforts that he was previously involved in. When I heard this story, it was poetic justice. As much as I despised Jong, that guy was a smart and resourceful communist.

Despite Klepto Man's flaws, and my conclusion that he is a severely lacking successful slacker, he has lasted for over three years due to his successful politics, moderate sales performance, and monumental bullshitting. He is a top-gun bullshitter, no doubt; one of the best I've seen. You almost want to believe him, even when you know he is full of it. He also got in good with Tigol Biddy, who is the grandmaster politico, and it has benefited him greatly. Even though he has made it despite the behavior, if it came down to firing either Klepto Man or a true successful slacker, Klepto Man will most likely take the walk. Learn from his mistakes. Perception is everything.

K.P.'s Notes

- Unfortunately, successful slackers must understand the game of corporate politics and play them in order to befriend the most savvy of political manipulators so they can protect you from scrutiny. Obviously, the higher up the better.

- Do not befriend more than one political guru; stick with the one you feel is the most influential and stay loyal to that person.

- Identify the highest overachievers in your peer group and associate yourself with them. However, approach with caution, because if your successful slacking game is not honed, they will sense it and blow your cover to management.

- Avoid being seen with unsuccessful slackers or disgruntled employees. Although they may be cool and anti-establishment, they will tarnish your image.

- In sales, seek out overachieving partners in order to boost your sales revenues and perception as a team player. Pass them deals to work and close so you can take long and uninterrupted breaks from work.

- Have customers who you've established good rapport with send e-mail messages highlighting your stellar customer service and worth to the company.

- In organizations which are disorganized or turbulent, sales quotas never have to be attained. A successful slacker's adjusted quota is normally between 70 and 85 percent of the quota established from management. The remaining 15 to 30 percent shortfall can be commonly blamed on a myriad of company problems.

- Establish ambiguous goals and commitments during annual reviews to maximize your likelihood of attaining them. If management presses for more accountability, tie your goals to the group so if you fall short the finger can be pointed elsewhere.

- KPIs (Key Performance Indicators) and other measures of worker productivity can be overcome by developing an intricate list of fake phone numbers in your territory and ones which stay connected until you hang up. On paper, you'll look like a hard-working employee, when in reality you're out riding your bike while the phone is still connected.

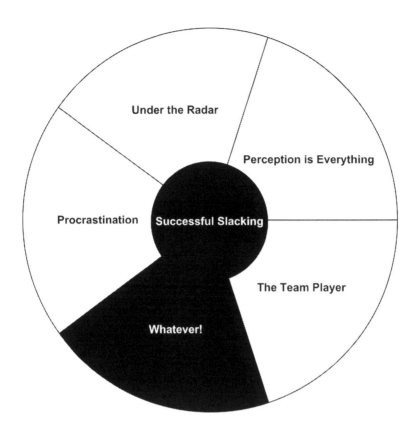

Under the Radar

Perception is Everything

Procrastination

Successful Slacking

The Team Player

Whatever!

Habit Two: Whatever!

"The key to life is adjustment."

My physical education teacher back in high school was a drunken, uneducated, and gullible woman in her late fifties who wore pink jogging suits and had those huge circular bifocals that were ever so popular in the mid-1970s. She never really taught me much beyond the fact that a teacher should never swig a handle of Wild Turkey before coming to school.

However, the one thing that has stuck with me all these years since I was in her health class is a term which is central to the second habit of a successful slacker: "The key to life is adjustment." Now, in her situation, this was probably most applicable at the liquor store when they ran out of Jack Daniel's, and she had to settle for Jimmy Beam. But regardless, the term is universal in its meaning and is closely related to the second habit, Whatever!

The Only Constant Is Change

Whatever! is a state of mind which is adopted once the successful slacker realizes that everything at work is much more enjoyable when you don't care. Because the ideal slacker job is within a turbulent company, changes happen more often than the official corporate stadium sponsor of the San Francisco Giants.

As soon as you get used to a certain process or routine, guess what? It's musical chairs time. Re-org everybody, yee haw! New territories, right on! How about a new office? Oh, you've only been in this one three weeks? No problem. Let's pick up all your shit and chuck it down the hall. Excuse me, sir, would you like to super-size that with a new manager? Okay! Oh, you aren't happy about quota? How about we raise it by 20 percent? Is that better? Stock performance has been stagnant for four years? What if we were to have leadership screw up so badly that our stock takes a thirty-point dip and wipe out all of your equity in the company? Would that be better? Here's a great idea: Let's hire a manager with absolutely no sales experience. Brilliant, my dear lad, brilliant!   This is just scratching the surface of all the incidents which cause the successful slacker to say *Whatever!*

As was mentioned earlier, in the last three years, I have had four managers. In addition to that, we have had five different VPs and four directors (with a new one on the way). In thirteen quarters, my territory and quota have changed about eight times, my office has been moved five times (including an entire building move), the job focus has gone from new business only, to new and existing, to only new in small companies, to only new in large companies, to new in both small and large, to named accounts with new small companies, to working new accounts alone, to teaming with field sales, to working against the partners, to working with the partners – phew! It goes on and on and on.

What kind of attitude perseveres in this environment? Not the guy with focus and dedication. Not the guy who likes to poach other people's deals. Not the guy who takes non-recoverable draws for three months and quits – although this is a good temporary strategy. The person who survives the longest is the one who can adapt the quickest and just say *Whatever!*

Laugh It Off

When decisions are made that make no sense or negatively affect you, there is little that can be done to alter them. As an employee, you have two choices: either deal with it or tender your resignation. It is easy to get angry at the decisions over which you have no control, but this anger can sometimes lead to comments and behavior that may tarnish your image. I have definitely fallen victim to it before, and continue to struggle in this arena. It is tough not to get angry when a co-worker with Virginia territory closes a deal in your patch and you find out about it after the fact, on your own investigations. It is even worse when management tries to justify the behavior and make excuses as to why it was okay, even though it was a blatant violation of the rules.

In these situations, laugh it off. Look at the ridiculousness of it all. There is a lot of humor in the asinine decisions that corporate leadership makes. As a successful slacker, you need to let go of the emotional and personal investment of time into the job. When there is an overriding *Whatever!* attitude, you can smile, leave your manager's office, have a good laugh, and go fishing for the rest of the day. There is not much to get angry about when you couldn't care less.

Cautious Carelessness

While the Whatever! attitude is essential in successful slacking, one must be very cautious in how it is perceived by others. The Whatever! attitude can be quite contagious, and an influential slacker can convert an entire team to a Whatever! persona in short time, especially if the organization is really turbulent. If management identifies you as the root of this behavior, it could get ugly. Therefore, take trepidation in conveying Whatever! If you have close friends or fellow successful slackers who already share the ideology in common, then it is okay. Just make sure that you are not spoiling too many "good apples" and making it evident to management.

Self-Realization

There are some people who you won't even need to lay the Whatever! attitude upon; the intelligent and perceptive ones adopt it on their own. A co-worker of mine started eight months ago and was one of the most overachieving new hires I had ever seen. This guy – we will call him Lincoln – would come in early, make a ton of phone calls, and stay late every day. His call metrics were making the rest of the team look really bad, especially me. Every five minutes, I'd hear him talking with another customer, while I hadn't spoken with a single living human since I arrived three hours earlier.

I was getting annoyed with Lincoln's exuberance, but must admit it was a tiny bit motivating.

After a couple of months, Lincoln's call metrics had sagged severely, as if he had transformed into a completely different person. I was excited that he might be open to adopting the successful slacker ideology, as he was a proven overachiever who seemingly softened up. There is great satisfaction in convincing an overachiever to convert, so I went to work. Within ten minutes of talking with him, I realized Lincoln was already there. All on his own, the Whatever! attitude had become the mantra. He saw the turbulence, the hopelessness, and the fact that Lester, our manager, was out of the office sick every other day. He had spent three months toiling and had nothing to show for it. Besides, if Lester wasn't here, then why the hell should he bother showing up? I had found a new ally in the quest to slack successfully.

Guiding Others

There are other types of co-workers who are naturally driven to succeed, but too proud to admit that the battle is futile. A perfect example of this was my good friend K-Rat. He started at the company about a year ago, and right from the start was a dedicated employee. K-Rat was determined to be successful, and overachieved the activity metrics every day. He cold called, got references, and demoed daily like a dedicated overachiever. There was only one problem: his territory.

K-Rat had Wyoming, Idaho, Montana, and *parts* of Colorado (not the good parts), and had a quota that was equivalent to mine in the Northeast. Starting on day one, K-Rat was gazing up Mount Everest all by himself. It would be nearly impossible to successfully hit quota in the territory he was given.

In the first six months, it did not discourage him, and his behavior was quite inspiring. It actually got me working at least four hours a day, which is a lot. K-Rat's deals were tiny and nebulous. The customers were one- and two-person shops that bitched and moaned about price all the time. With his average deal size, K-Rat calculated that he would have to do forty deals in a quarter to hit his target. The most I have ever seen anyone close in the three years I had done the job was thirty-five. K-Rat was realizing the peril of his situation. Even though failure loomed, K-Rat was – as management says – "in it to win it."

He worked the same territory for almost a year, and because the commission structure had a 60 percent threshold, he would not make anything extra unless he brought in at least that amount of his number. Due to the insanity of K-Rat's quota, he never hit 60 percent in four attempts. He came very close, but never got a commission check in almost a year. It was really sad to see, because K-Rat thought of himself as a failure, even though the organization and leadership was the true failure.

They did not take into consideration his territory. They gave better territories to other people who had been hired six months after him, even though he continually asked for a new one. He looked for help and assistance, but his manager, Tigol Biddy, just gave him a blank stare, shared a mindless equestrian reference to Seattle Slew and Seabiscuit, and said "Keep working hard, you'll make it!"

Halfway through his tenure, I started injecting the Whatever! attitude into K-Rat. He needed it for peace of mind and sanity. I suggested a weeklong vacation, but he was too nervous that he might get in trouble with Tigol Biddy. Meanwhile, I was calling in sick for an entire week to go hang out with my buddy in Arizona. I led by example and guided him down the path of sanity so he could adopt Whatever! and have much more fun at work.

After about eight months, he had finally made the change. K-Rat took sick time and vacations, he sent me URL links all day to interesting news stories, we took two-hour lunches together, he taught me how to start a business on eBay, and we both called in sick one day to go drive our cars at Laguna Seca. It was so rewarding to see K-Rat adopt the philosophy. His attitude improved, and he was more jovial than I had ever seen him.

Within another two months, he told me he was quitting the next day. K-Rat had found a job only three miles from home and was getting the same base pay, better commission, and the entire Eastern Seaboard as a territory. Although I was sad to see him leave, it felt good to know that I was able to guide him down the path to

Whatever! It enriched his life for a while, and led K-Rat to a better opportunity. I hope that in the future, K-Rat will self-realize – as Lincoln did – that when the situation is without hope, Whatever! is the only path to sanity.

Lessons to Be Learned from Mud Boy

Before my current downer of a manager, Les, there was a guy by the name of Mud Boy. Mud Boy was probably the coolest manager I've ever had, because he was a walking persona of the Whatever! attitude. For a manager, this is a rare gift. He had Jimmy Buffett posters in his office, would take long lunch breaks to go golfing, and his computer wallpaper was the sixteenth (I think) hole of Pebble Beach Golf Course. He was a slacker's slacker and a super-cool guy to hang with, and he looked like a mix between Harry Connick, Jr. and Ray Romano. I'd even have an occasional pinch of Skoal in his office during our **one-on-one**. God, those times were great. I regret that we weren't closer, but golfing was his main thing, and I am not a golf guy.

Anyway, Mud Boy was getting along at the company just fine as a manager within our group. He had gotten the job because two years prior, he was involved in an acquisition that brought him to the corporate behemoth. Therefore, his acquisition experience could help bring insight to our recently acquired group. He went through the first six months coasting and looking relatively relaxed.

As year-end drew closer, I could see the pressure coming down on him. Then one day, Mud Boy decided to go directly against his mantra of Whatever! It was a mistake that cost him dearly.

A few months before the end of the year, we were far behind our number, as usual. Mud Boy, who was in charge of managing the East Coast inside-sales team, had to work with a guy we will call Scrote (you probably can guess why) who was responsible for the East Coast field team. Scrote was the antithesis of Mud Boy. He was an overachieving manager, and would act like your best buddy one day, only to gore you the next with a dull butter knife. Not to mention he looked like a cartoon character with a nose so long it could be used for alpine ski jumping and hair so finely combed with Brylcreem, you could see his scalp through each individual line of hair. Oh, he also smelled like a dirty, smoky bar from huffing on cancer sticks all day.

Back to the story: Leadership was scrutinizing the East Coast team, and asked why we were so far behind the number. Scrote predictably started pointing the finger at our group. Mud Boy got irritated, because he had the numbers in **black and white** to prove Scrote was wrong. However, Scrote was a longtime employee of the acquired company, and for whatever ungodly reason, leadership listened to him. Mud Boy came to me one day and showed me the e-mail where Scrote called out our team as the problem. Mud Boy was visibly annoyed.

"Well, do you have proof to back up our innocence?" I asked.

"Hell yeah," Mud Boy replied. "I got it all documented in a spreadsheet. It shows that our group produces more revenue than Scrote's team."

"Well then, defend yourself," I said.

It seemed as though Mud Boy was in the right. He would be able to make a stand and finally knock Scrote down to who he really was. I was excited to hopefully see a successful slacker build his own positive perception and take out the underhanded overachiever.

At this point, another interesting character, Dolt, came into play. Dolt was new to the organization and came in as the director and manager of Mud Boy and Scrote. I have no idea how Dolt got the position, but it may have been because he dazzled his interviewers with dopey terms like **soup to nuts** and **green pastures.** Describing Dolt is simple. Think of Butthead. Okay, now picture his long face and wafty brown hair with that goofy expression and a muttering of "uh huh huh huh." Now pretend Butthead is twenty years older and an actual person without braces. This is Dolt, no joking.

Mud Boy went to Dolt because he felt that Scrote was being unfair and accusatory. In typical Dolt fashion, he refused to listen to Mud Boy's case because he was somehow mesmerized by the unexplainable draw of Scrote. Now that I think about it, Scrote does resemble Beavis quite a bit, with the long nose and raspy smoker's voice.

Mud Boy was stuck. Here he was being accused of not producing, when in fact it was Scrote's team who was not. Mud Boy even had documentation to back it up, but Dolt would not listen to his case. At this point, Mud Boy should have realized the futility, thrown the papers up in the air, and said Whatever! Chances are, after a few weeks, everyone would have forgotten about the whole incident – being behind the number was a common occurrence. Instead, Mud Boy decided to push onward and prove that he was right.

Mud Boy went above Dolt's head and directly to the VP of our business group, "Small" Paul Bunyan. Now Small Bunyan was the golden boy of the acquisition. He was the CEO's right-hand man, and after the deal with the acquiring giant, the startup CEO made sure Small Bunyan was sitting pretty – and he was. To enhance your image of him, imagine a short Rob Lowe/Tom Cruise with a stubbly beard and an intense case of short man's complex.

Mud Boy went to Small Bunyan and presented his case that Scrote was wrongly accusing him and that Dolt would not listen. Here is the kicker: Small Bunyan, being an important and busy VP, replied to Mud Boy, *attached* Dolt with the e-mail Mud Boy sent, and told Mud Boy he should discuss the situation with Dolt. Nail in the coffin, folks. Dolt called Mud Boy into his office and said "Mud Boy, what you did, it wasn't very smart." My manager, Mud Boy, had stepped himself into a monstrosity of dung. At that point, he was basically done as a manager and employee.

The next quarter, Mud Boy had been demoted to a sales rep. They gave him a territory and no time to get trained, ramped up on the technology, or even build his pipeline. Within three months, they had fired Mud Boy. It was a shame and further proof to me that the Whatever! attitude must be a key part of the successful slacker's persona. Without it, one may erroneously stand up for what is right and get fired for it. I just hope he filed a lawsuit against the company. I feel partly responsible for Mud Boy's demise, because after his unsuccessful initial meeting with Dolt, he came and asked my opinion.

"Go to Small Bunyan," I said. "He is a numbers guy. If you are concise and have figures to back up your argument, he will listen to you."

"You think so?" Mud Boy responded.

"Definitely."

I honestly didn't try to set Mud Boy up. I wanted to help him win the battle against Scrote, because he stole a large deal of mine less than a year prior. It was a lesson for both of us, but more for Mud Boy. He is better off anyway. Mud Boy is probably at home in Santa Cruz, golfing and working at a way more relaxed and enjoyable company. At least I hope he is.

K.P.'s Notes

- Learn from my drunken high school physical education teacher – the key to life is adjustment. Successful slackers learn to cope with the ever-changing atmosphere inside disorganized and bureaucratically stifled corporations.

- When you couldn't care less about what happens at work, things like cubicle moves, reorganizations, quota increases, five different managers in a year, a thirty-point plummet in stock value, and the criminal prosecution of the CEO have no impact on your life beyond a laugh and a conversation topic with customers.

- When you've mistakenly invested significant effort into a project meant to help the organization, only to see it squashed before your eyes, laugh it off and learn not to waste your time in the future.

- Approach the Whatever! attitude with cautious carelessness. If management picks up on your overriding lack of concern for anything related to the company, it will negatively affect your perception as a dedicated employee.

- Although some astute overachievers will eventually realize that hard work is futile and conclude on their own the need to adopt Slackism, others may need help. Take time to guide the less perceptive toward a prosperous life of successful slacking.

- Learn from Mud Boy and don't fight for what you think is right when management scrutinizes you. Even with documented proof that you aren't to blame, if the political machine is in full effect, you'll still take the fall for speaking your mind. Say and do nothing, and eventually the whole debacle will blow over and be forgotten.

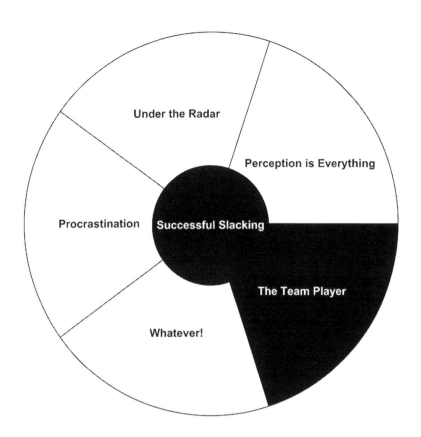

Habit Three: The Team Player

"Many people quit looking for work when they find a job."

Management will put up with people who are less productive employees if others like them, they are easy to work with and manage, and are team players. Because the successful slacker is naturally going to be less productive than others, they must be disciplined in the team player department. The **impetus** to achieving this goal is to remember that people must enjoy your company and persona. If nobody is stopping by your office or cube to chitchat, you aren't doing a good enough job of being a good team player.

Avoid Uber-Team Playing

Every company has a few people who are the suck-ups or **brown-nosers**. These folks have existed since the beginning of time. You remember little Johnny or Sally who would always bring the teacher a shiny red apple? Yeah, well those Eddie Haskell types are all grown up now and are still brimming with more kaka than a port-a-john at an Irritable Bowel Syndrome convention. Many consider these people to be the team players because they want everyone to like them. They are desperate to climb the **corporate ladder** and strive to be the one that everybody on the team turns to in a time of need. Successful slackers couldn't care less about being a team player, but in order to build the façade, it is a role that is essential.

As a successful slacker, it's not necessary to go over the top as a team player like Johnny or Sally often do – think of it as a more passive rather than active role. You will never outdo an overachiever, and probably don't care to, so refuse to compete with them. Be a team player by doing personal favors, being easy to work with and talk to, never saying "I can't" or "I won't" when somebody asks you to do something, and occasionally back up your manager on items which you feel may be remotely important. Don't feel like you have to be the cheerleader or the source of inspiration for the team. That isn't your job. Your job is to advance perception and image through being a person who is easy to talk, work, and relate with individually.

Connect on a Personal Level

The successful slacker has a myriad of leisure activities that have far more importance compared to work. Therefore, it is easy for the successful slacker to ask teammates about their free-time endeavors and get some lively and meaningful conversation out of it. You may quickly find a lot in common, so use this to help further the relationship. Always listen more than talk. Remember the hobbies and interests of each individual on the team, and if you bump into them in the hallway, focus a conversation around those activities.

If you discover there are co-workers whose main hobby is work, distance yourself. These are lost souls who will potentially either make your job as a team player really hard, or they will be too much effort to strike a common chord with. Keep the conversations light and distant, and occasionally send them an e-mail about something work-related which may be of benefit.

If a co-worker comes to you with a question, always try to get an answer. Personal favors take priority over everything, and provided the questions aren't too outlandish, do your best to get the answer quickly. Before long, there will be several people on the team asking you questions. Although this may seem like a hassle on the surface, what it is doing is advancing rapport with the team members and building your image as a team player.

Lester Wurth, the Manager

My manager, Lester Wurth, and I went back a few years to when we were both sales reps. He actually started at a lower level than I did, but eventually became my manager through his quintessential overachieving and absolutely zero life or personality. He also kissed Tigol Biddy's ass, which accelerated his **trending** toward management status. Because of this odd work dynamic, we had a strange relationship. It was almost a mutual respect for one another, but not really. He was a good sales rep, but as a manager, he was absolutely atrocious – worse than atrocious.

Les had no charisma, provided no inspiration, offered little help or assistance, and nobody liked talking to him. None of his **core competencies** qualified him to be an effective manager. The only thing he knew how to do well was unleash expletives when upset and tell his sales reps to "just close it." He even bought us all baseball caps with the term "Git-R-Done" on the front, made famous by Larry the Cable Guy. It was a kind yet pathetic gesture, and we needed far more motivation incentive than a baseball cap with a clichéd slogan on it. (However, it did make quite a nice birthday re-gift for my brother!)

Les was only in his late twenties, but he was getting wrinkles from excessive smoking and drinking, and grey hairs from letting stress get to him. From his physical appearance, you'd think he was ten years older. From the time he was a sales rep to the time he was a manager, it looked as if he put on more than twenty pounds of weight. Les had health issues so frequently that he was out of the office sick several days of nearly every month. Usually, the sickness came on during month- and quarter-end, when being in the office is most critical.

It must have been the mounting stress and the endless days of toil which made him yet another victim of work-related mental and physical breakdown. In his futile quest to achieve management excellence, Les employed the most belabored corporate terms and had an uncanny ability to fit several of them in just one sentence. I think he acquired the skill from his mentor, Tigol Biddy. One time he came and knocked on my door.

"Hey Les, come on in!" I said, after checking that my phone was disconnected. Les entered with his typical mopey look, beer gut, and hunched-over shoulders.

"So, have we heard back from Prophecy Corporation yet?"

He always smelled really bad, like a mix between mothballs and cigarettes. I would back away in my chair to escape the stench.

"Yeah, I sent you an e-mail," I responded.

"Really? I don't remember seeing it," said Les.

"Are you sure? I sent it to your Wurth.Les e-mail address. Basically, the deal is stalled another two weeks," I replied.

"SHIT! Aww…fuck! Dammit! Well, just get it done. Close the business."

"Right. That's pretty obvious," I said.

"I can't express to you in words how dire our situation is," bellowed Les. "We need to do everything possible to **ratchet up** the metrics, **prioritize,** and **circle back** with customers to get the deals **squared away**."

The corporate geometric references were akin to fingernails being run down a chalkboard.

"Right, you said that yesterday," I responded.

"I know," said Les. "But I just want to **touch base** again so that we are **locked and loaded** to close out the quarter on an upward trend. Achoo Bleseu is **poking holes** in our pipeline reports."

"Yeah, right, I get it. Anything else?"

"Just close business," he muttered.

This was the kind of insightful leadership we dealt with on a daily basis. I sat for a moment in shock. After digesting the comment, I turned and picked up the "Git-R-Done" hat, put it on crooked, stood up to get in a squatting position, hiked up my jeans, craned out my neck, pointed both my fingers at the hat and said in my best Arkansas accent, "Do you mean, GIT-R-DONE?!" I don't think he saw the value add in my question.

Les was berated by Achoo Bleseu's metrics and pipeline inquisitions, which also drove him to fits of profanity and the frequent sick days. Achoo was metrics man, and he poked more holes in KPI reports than the Illinois Enema Bandit poked his co-ed victims. Never mind closing deals, Achoo only cared about how many calls were made in a day and how many hours of talk time were completed.

Next to Les, I was the second most senior person on the team. Therefore, most new hires came to me asking for help, because either Les was in meetings with Achoo or out sick. Most often, it was simply because they couldn't handle the droning and cussing of our fearless leader. It was the perfect opportunity to build my reputation as an effective team player.

The situation was also ideal for Les, because I was taking a lot of diversions and work off of his hands. He was too busy getting tongue-lashed by Achoo every day to spend time working with his direct reports and building a meaningful relationship with them. I was able to build the façade of a selfless team player while not taking on any more responsibility or workload – and I was making friends.

However, take caution with this behavior, because there are some of those psycho power-hungry types like Kim Jong Il who want all of the attention. If you are stealing your manager's time with his or her subordinates, and the manager is a certified crackpot, you could end up being in big trouble.

Value-add E-mails

As a solid team player, be sure that you are sending helpful e-mails to the team at least once or twice a month. Don't overindulge, because the corporate brown-noser will send at least a couple per week, which is far too many, and you don't want to build that reputation. In addition, the information brown-nosers send is usually not critical or even relevant. If people come to you after sending an e-mail, saying things like "Hey, thanks for the article," or "Man, I didn't realize that," the information you are sending is quality. Always include your manager on the e-mail, of course, and if you are feeling really saucy, attach your manager's manager if the information is relevant enough.

There are also other kinds of e-mail which are beneficial for your image as a team player. Instead of work-related e-mails, if you come across an article about how to do a new trick called the "kick-flip double-fakey triple-bypass rimjob," and your co-worker is an avid skateboarder, send the URL link to him. There is a possibility he's never seen it before and may graciously thank you for thinking of him. Being a team player is more than just doing work-related favors, so remember the leisure interests of your co-workers. Who knows, you may actually score a few really good friends outside of work from it.

In a sales environment, a particularly effective use of e-mail is to forward leads on to other sales reps and attach any necessary managers. In the ideal job, change and turbulence is the only constant, so chances are your territory gets flipped every quarter or so. If this is the case, and you have a bunch of opportunities which are no longer technically yours, don't waste time unless they are truly close to closing.

Take this opportunity to pass them on to the new rep. Poaching and holding out accounts for excessive periods of time will only hurt your team-player image. Besides, do you really want all that extra work? It is so liberating to get a bunch of stagnant accounts off your plate and focus on Internet poker all the while building positive perception.

Apply for Jobs in which You Are Underqualified

In the process of writing The Five Habits, I had applied for a team lead position. Usually, slackers would not do something like this, but the successful slacker knows when getting the job is attainable or when the competition is too fierce. Realizing the other applicants were mostly overachievers and cheerleaders, the likelihood of me getting the job was slim to none, regardless of how well I interviewed. So why even waste time?

In order to build the perception of a good team player, the successful slacker makes efforts, however half-assed they may be, to show management the dedication and commitment to career advancement. My chances were nominal, which made it even more important to apply. What would have happened if I actually got the job? I most likely would have turned it down, which would have raised a case of **FUD** in management's mind.

Questions would arise like: Is he having second thoughts? I thought he was a team player and committed to his career? Why would he turn down such a great opportunity? Turning down a job only puts the successful slacker dead center on the radar screen, which is to be avoided at all costs. Just this morning, Achoo Bleseu came into my office to talk. At first, I was a little worried about why he was coming to speak with me, since he never stopped by.

"I wanted to circle back regarding the team lead job," he said.

"Oh, great!" I responded with hollow enthusiasm.

"We apologize for not keeping you **in the loop**, but a few of us were **out of pocket** on vacation, and it was tough to assemble a **quorum** and make the decision."

"No problem," I said.

"We thank you for applying," Right at that moment, a big load was lifted, as I knew the job went to someone else. "But we felt there were a few other candidates who were a little bit more qualified."

Never before had I felt so **empowered**. Here was the director of our organization, trying to gently break the news, while I was doing the Macarena with my hands and feet under the desk. The plan had worked to perfection. Achoo Bleseu shared the reasons why I didn't get the job, and encouraged me to keep up the good work and improve in a few areas. One of those areas happened to be consistency in quota attainment, which I found strange. If anything, I was the most consistent **SSP** in the organization – I always came in between 70 and 85 percent. You could set a watch to it! Regardless, the whole scenario turned out to be far more beneficial than anticipated. Achoo Bleseu shared more good news which made me jump out of my seat.

"We appreciate your continued commitment and realize you have talked with us about salary and **grade level** adjustment. You will be happy to learn of the changes during your annual review with Les."

It was a happy day, a very happy day. A few months prior, I had made multiple comments about my salary being at a lower grade level compared to new folks who had come into the organization after the acquisition. Achoo Bleseu officially recognized my repeated requests, so I am now awaiting my adjusted salary and grade. How is that for building the team player façade? I apply for a job, don't get it, but get a pay raise anyway. More pay for the same or lesser amount of work is like winning the gold medal at the Slacker Olympics. The pinnacle has been attained!

The Sick Team Player

As a successful slacker, sickness can come in many different forms: influenza, allergies, whooping cough, dehydration, bibliomania, diarrhea, anything with the suffix -itis, heavy period flow (women have a *huge* advantage with this one), mono, enuresis, pink eye, panic attacks, or the more trendy West Nile virus and mad cow disease – the list is only limited by one's imagination. The true ailment most successful slackers suffer from is sickness of work. It is nauseating to be at the helm of a computer and phone all day.

Everyone has called in sick at least one time when they were not really in bed with the cold. The successful slacker is usually sick more often than his co-workers, but in the spirit of being a team player, the successful slacker makes sure that resentment doesn't build inside the team.

It is achieved by checking e-mail every few hours, having an updated **OOF message**, and **pinging** people to make it look like you are actually at home sick and caring. It can be a pain in the ass, especially if you are out waterskiing, mountaineering, or paragliding. It's tough to access a computer, but it's critical that this advice be followed. If you call in sick, and nobody hears from you all day, resentment and doubt can build, which will affect perception as a team player. However, if you call a few people and send e-mails sporadically, it really proves the level of dedication. It is admirable when someone with spinal meningitis is still devoted enough to get work done.

When calling in sick to your manager, either leave a voicemail or send an e-mail early in the morning. Don't do it the night before; that's far more suspect. It's way more believable when the call comes at six or seven in the morning. Call before your manager gets into the office, so that it seems you made an effort to come in, but just can't seem to make it out the door.

For all you successful slackers out there with wireless e-mail devices, don't use them! When an e-mail is sent, it usually shows up saying "This e-mail was sent from my 'so-and-so' wireless device" at the bottom of the e-mail for advertising purposes. The excuse "But I was at the doctor's office" does not fly. Besides, what the hell are you doing with a wireless e-mail device? Successful slackers use those pieces of crap as paperweights or props at work only to look busy.

Foreshadowing Sickness

Another tactic employed is foreshadowing sickness. There was a short-notice mountain bike trip my buddies were going on, which required me to take two days off work. After just getting back from a weeklong vacation, it would be hard to get more official time off. So the day before the trip, I telegraphed sickness in a one on one meeting with Les. I started making fake sneezes and drying my eyes while sniffling. He was in the middle of maundering about pipeline when I fake sneezed really loud and interrupted him.

"Are you okay?" he asked.

"Ah, yeah. I think. Damn allergies, they're killing me," I responded.

"Yeah, I know the feeling. Hope you get better."

"Thanks Les. I'm fighting through it, man. Gotta get work done though," I said.

"Well, I appreciate your dedication."

I foreshadowed an oncoming sickness, so that when the call came the following morning, he was not all that surprised or suspicious. The beauty of it was that the following two days, he was sick as well, so the timing couldn't have worked out better. Successful slacking requires top-notch acting. It makes your façade all the more believable.

Another time I used the excuse of taking a nasty spill in a bike race. I was out for a few days, but upon my return, the evidence of the fall had to somehow be there. I limped around the office for the following three days or so, especially in the midst of my old manager Mud Boy. I told him about the fabricated accident, and he asked to see the cuts (just out of curiosity), but I told them they were way up my leg, and I didn't think pulling my pants down was appropriate. The conversation ended right there. I knew he didn't really care either way, but I figured it was good acting practice in case I ever had a manager like Kim Jong Il.

Interview and Hire Successful Slackers

The successful slacker is a rare breed and is not easy to identify on the surface. Corporations need successful slackers as much as they need overachievers. Therefore, in the interest of being a team player, offer management your assistance in candidate interviews. Getting involved with this process ensures that a steady flow of successful slackers enters the work environment. Use discretion in how many you recommend to hire. It is not good for your image if there is hyper-saturation of successful slackers. They may steal your thunder. However, it is always good to have a few allies working in the company.

Once the interview commences, immediately ask them how their SAA process is coming along. If they respond with "on track" or "off track," then there is a winner candidate in your midst. It doesn't matter which response, the mere indication they said either of those terms qualifies them as an aspiring successful slacker. If they give a blank expression, you either have a complete rookie or an overachiever in the room. If the candidate is a rookie, it will be easy selling them on the merits of successful slacking. An overachiever will be much harder, so bring your A-game, and an unsuccessful slacker, well, we know about them.

Ask questions like: "Tell me about your busiest time last year. What made it so busy? How were you able to overcome this and still put your leisure activities first?"; "Tell me about a scenario that got you extremely frustrated. How did you deal with it? Were you still able to leave work early with a clear mind, as to not ruin your afternoon leisure activities?"; "In which areas could you improve time management skills so that when co-workers take you on a two-hour lunch, you can still leave by three o'clock?"

These types of questions will really uncover the worth of a candidate. Focus at least one around each of The Five Habits. As a team player, you are doing yourself a favor by getting successful slackers hired and improving your image as a helpful and willing employee. If the candidate does well with each response, prep them on the interviews they will have in the future, so they do well and have a better chance of success.

Interview Attire

Be cognizant of what you wear on the day the interviews occur. Just this morning, Les called me into his office and said, "**On a go-forward basis**, it would better if you didn't wear shorts and a T-shirt on a candidate interview day." After looking at my attire, and then looking at his, I responded.

"So jeans and a T-shirt are more appropriate?"

It was not meant to be a condescending retort – okay, maybe slightly – but seriously, a guy wearing jeans telling me that my attire isn't appropriate? The best part was what he said next: "It may give the candidate the wrong impression. We both know that it's all about perception." I was floored. He admitted the first habit of successful slackers as if he had pre-read my book before I even wrote it.

"Oh yes," I replied, "perception is everything. Indeed."

I went back to my office with a grin wider than the grille of a '57 El Dorado. God forbid I give the candidate the wrong impression. We don't want him to find out that this is **R3BC** disguised as a legitimate, organized, and efficient business. What about my attire? As was mentioned earlier, it is pretty hard to go play Frisbee golf in jeans or dress pants. I rode my bike to work on this particular day and didn't feel like bringing the old slacks along.

I walked into the interview, and the guy was sitting there in a three-piece suit with a tie. I was wearing a Hawaiian T-shirt, Billabong shorts, and sandals. He stared at me, and with an embarrassed look, he said, "Oh, wow, uh, I guess I am a little overdressed."

"Nah, I'm probably underdressed, but whatever!"

I wanted to give this guy the right impression, not the wrong one. Yes, I am wearing shorts. Yes, we all wear shorts here. Who in their right mind would be turned off by wearing shorts? It is like being on vacation, only at work.

Wearing shorts in an interview is the fastest way to determine whether or not the candidate will be a good fit. If they are turned off by shorts, there is nothing left to say but "Thanks for coming out, guy. Good luck." You do not want someone like that on your team. Everybody loves wearing shorts. If somebody says they don't, they are either lying, they are obscenely fat, or they have an unsightly leg growth which makes them self-conscious.

Lessons to Be Learned from Swindla

If there was any person at my old company who exemplified anti-team-player attitude, it was a woman we will refer to as Swindla. Swindla was one of the shadiest and most mentally disturbed employees I've ever seen. Even though her appearance was unassuming – five feet tall and about one hundred pounds, Indian descent, seemingly soft-spoken – Swindla's reputation preceded her.

She had been hired from the chief competitor, and other recent hires who came from the same company knew that Swindla was a certified nutcase who had no sales experience, compulsively lied, and was a scam artist. In addition to those redeeming qualities, her dirty mouth made a sailor seem like a choirboy. Swindla would drop an F-bomb about as frequently as she would breathe.

She had the pleasure of being on Kim Jong Il's team, and the true pleasure came from watching these two go at it. Because Swindla was such a raging bitch, and Jong was a corporate Commie, he would not stand for the insubordination. He would go into her office and have discussions regarding all the fake phone calls she was making to pad her metrics. The conversations went something like this, and folks, this is not exaggeration.

"Hey Swindla, **FYI**, I noticed you've been making phone calls to San Jose area code all day, but your territory is Texas. What gives?"

"Get off my fucking back, Jong. I am sick of you fucking nagging me."

"Excuse me? I am your manager, don't ever talk to me like that."

"You're not my fucking manager, you're a fucking JOKE!"

"HEY! WATCH YOUR GODDAMN MOUTH!"

"FUCK YOU, JONG!"

"FUCK YOU!"

At this point, people would start gathering in the hallways to have a listen in on the two lovebirds. Nobody could believe their eyes and ears. It was not a casual conversation, but a full-on screaming match. My old company prides themselves on hiring only the most productive employees. Well, I guess they hired Swindla on the merits of her ability to productively fit thirty F-bombs within a one-minute conversation. That *is* quite productive, if you ask me. To all of you aspiring successful slackers, it should be obvious that this behavior is not becoming of a team player. Never, under any circumstances, do you drop F-bombs in front of your manager, unless you have a tight relationship.

While we are on the topic of Swindla, let's discuss the behavior which earned her the alias. Yes, she did curse a lot, but she was even more successful in scamming the company out of approximately six months of pay. How did Swindla achieve this feat? Well, first off, she had a lot of practice, because I found out that she learned the scam at her previous employer. One day, she came to work on crutches and a cast. The story was that she broke her foot, which I can't validate as true or false. What I do know is that after a month, the crutches were gone. She would walk in with the obligatory limp, have a nice morning expletive session with Jong, and then hobble on home at the end of the day.

After a few weeks, she wasn't coming into the office any longer, but was still an employee. I asked around and discovered that she swindled a medical excuse, which stipulated she was physically unable to work and was entitled up to 60 percent of full-pay income until she was fit to return. Apparently, she had to have surgery on a bunion, which affected her health and ability to perform her job function – a bunion, folks. She works inside sales. How the hell does that make *any* sense whatsoever? Logical or not, this foul-mouthed fib-master got at least four months' pay for taking a vacation.

Some people may see this as a master tactic for the successful slacker. Although Swindla did achieve quite an impressive feat – and I have to admit jealousy – there was no way in hell the company would keep her as an employee upon returning. Sure enough, a few months ago, I saw her tottering in the hallway saying her final goodbyes. Upon my approach to say farewell, I stepped on her ugly-ass foot and made her cry and curse me out. Okay I didn't, but damn, it would have been quite gratifying.

K.P.'s Notes

- Management will put up with employees who are less productive, as long as they are well-liked, easy to manage, and are team players.

- In order to be an effective team player, the Ferris Bueller effect must be honed so that co-workers and management like you.

- Team playing should be used to help advance perception and image through being a person who is easy to talk, work, and relate with on a personal level.

- Have meaningful conversations with co-workers and take a genuine interest in their leisure-time activities. If they have no leisure activities, or their only enjoyment is work, distance yourself. These are lost souls who cannot be saved.

- By helping new hires and other people on your team, you'll take some of the burden off your manager, and improve your worth as an employee, even though you contribute far less than the rest of the team.

- Occasionally send work-related value-add e-mails to the team and your manager, in order to maintain your image. If you come across Web sites or articles related to your co-workers' hobbies, share them as well.

- Apply for jobs for which you are underqualified. Your chances of getting the position will be low, but it will show that you are making efforts – however half-assed they may be – toward improving your career path within the company.

• When faking sickness as successful slackers often do, always check e-mail and respond to voicemails to appear devoted. It may be a hassle, especially when you're out hang gliding, but it will reaffirm your commitment to the company.

• When out sick, never send e-mails from wireless devices like a Wackberry. The excuse that you were at the doctor's office does not fly. Besides, successful slackers only use those digerati devices as paperweights or props to seem busy.

• Foreshadow sickness by coughing or other displays of illness. It will make your eventual absence from the office all the more believable.

• By being a team player, you'll eventually be involved in the interview process for new hires. Identify and hire successful slackers by asking key questions like: "Tell me about a scenario that got you extremely frustrated. How did you deal with it? Were you still able to leave work early with a clear mind as to not ruin your afternoon leisure activities?"

• When interviewing candidates, dress how you would normally dress at work. Don't give candidates the wrong impression about the company. If you normally wear a T-shirt, shorts, and sandals to work, continue to do so.

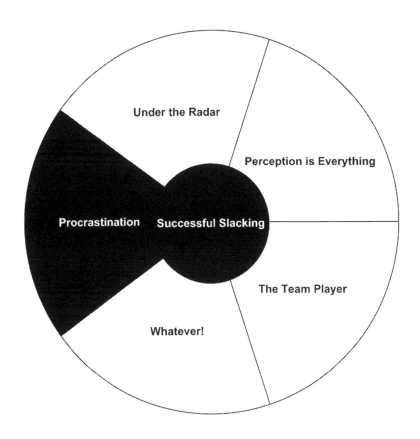

Habit Four: Procrastination

"Never put off till tomorrow what can be put off till the day after tomorrow."

- Mark Twain

Procrastination is a common trait, regardless of whether or not one is a successful slacker. I have known a great number of overachievers who were the most hardcore of procrastinators. They enjoyed working under stress and a **hard stop** deadline. It made them turn out better work, knowing that there was a **drop dead point**. In college, my wife was a perfect example of this. She would wait until midnight to write a five-page paper, only eight hours before it was due. She thrived on the looming pressure. Successful slackers do procrastinate, but not because they like the pressure; they do it to enhance their leisure time and perception within the team.

ACTION REQUIRED – Not Really

The successful slacker never completes a project or task ahead of schedule, unless there is some overriding reason why they should. This hardly ever happens, but when it does, it could be attributed to a reward of extra vacation time or free passes to the indoor go-kart track. Inside my company, if something needed to get done really quickly, the sender would put in the subject header **"ACTION REQUIRED."**

Yes, it is in all caps, so that nobody can use the excuse "Oh, I didn't realize this was a required action." To most people, the action required e-mail will get them immediately **on task**, especially those who are submissive. If they receive another e-mail or call following up to ask why it was not completed, they sweat profusely and get distraught, fearing their job may be in jeopardy. Not the successful slacker. Below is a **flowchart** that visually defines the process.

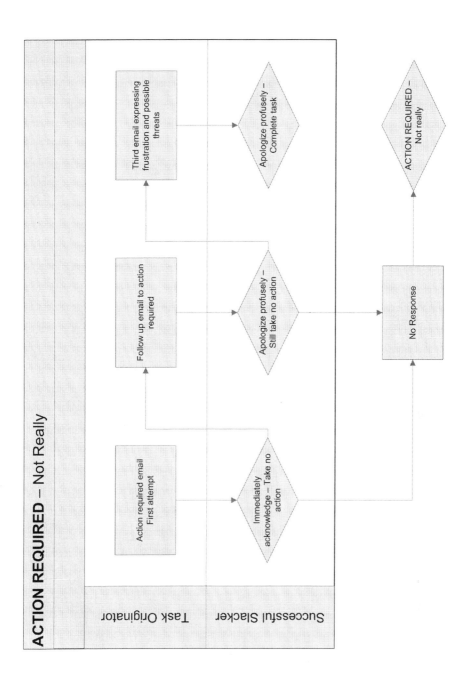

Figure 4: ACTION REQUIRED – Not Really

The successful slacker does not complete any assignments, whether it is action required or not, without at least three e-mails from the person who **owns** the task. The successful slacker responds immediately to the first e-mail and tells the person they are on it. That response makes the task owner feel at ease because the successful slacker was so quick in responding. After that, nothing gets done about the situation. If there is no follow-up by the owner, the successful slacker concludes that the issue is no longer urgent.

If there is a second e-mail or call from the owner, the slacker apologizes profusely. It makes the owner feel reassured that the slacker may have had some other important work-related issue to handle (not true), and will complete the task immediately. If at this point, there is no further follow-up, obviously, the successful slacker forgets about it.

If there is a third follow-up, it is wise to get the task completed in a somewhat short timeframe. I say *somewhat* because if you are actually writing a book, or taking a long lunch to go surfing (not on the Web), or whatnot, this task may potentially derail any leisure plans that were already set. However, the successful slacker makes sure that at least by the end of the week, maybe the end of the day, the task gets completed.

Once the task is complete, always be apologetic. The originator of the task may be annoyed that it took constant follow-up, but the fact you were responsive and apologetic will take care of that problem. Remember, people are more willing to put up with lower productivity and competence if an individual is well-liked, fits into the team, and is easy to manage.

Some may think "Wouldn't it just be easier to do the task the first time and get it over with?" Although that may seem obvious, the successful slacker realizes that a lot of times, people assign tasks they say are urgent which have no urgency whatsoever. They are either too paranoid or lazy to do the task themselves, and they usually try and pin it on someone else. In addition, if you complete the task immediately, the next time something similar comes up, who is the first person they will turn to? Being interrupted from your afternoon bike ride once in a week is bad enough, but two times? No way, Jose.

With the successful slacker methodology, people think that you are extremely busy, because it takes a few follow-ups to get something completed. The successful slacker apologizes and eventually gets it done, but always references the other work that was going on to delay the response. Next time, the originator may not turn to you because they realize you are overloaded and may take too much time in completing their urgent task. This behavior will significantly decrease the number of calls and e-mails you get to complete so-called "urgent" issues. Before long, you will leave the office for about a week of vacation, maybe more, and when you return, there will only be about thirty or so unread inbox e-mails.

Procrastination Creates Heroes

Have you ever been to a baseball game where somebody hits a grand slam home run in the bottom of the second inning? Was it exhilarating? I am sure it was exciting, but did it keep you on the edge of your seat or make you explode into wild hullabaloo? Now, take that same grand slam and put it at the bottom of the ninth inning with two outs and a full count. How much more exhilarating is that? There is no contest! You can cut the tension with a laser pointer. The entire stadium goes batshit and people throw beer on one another. The successful slacker understands this concept, and this is the exact reason why procrastination is one of The Five Habits.

In sales, if you bring in a huge, whopping deal at the beginning of a quarter, is it all that impressive? Yeah, it is probably nice and you feel good about it. People congratulate you, and within a week, forget about it. What if you brought in that same monstrous deal at the last minute of the last day of the year? All of a sudden, you become the salesman of the year, the new hot prospect, the hero everyone talks about. Nobody mentions the fact that you didn't close diddly-squat the entire quarter. They forget as soon as you land the whopper.

Procrastination can take the same exact deal from impressive to unbelievable. You left everybody in suspense the entire time. Some rooted for you, some hoped it didn't happen, but either way, there was tension and anticipation, just like at the bottom of the ninth inning with Casey taking the plate. Of course, it doesn't always work out to be a big win. Sometimes it works out to be a huge loss. But that is the gamble the successful slacker takes. As long as the wins outweigh the losses, you can remain at 1 Slack Street, Slackerville, MO, U.S.A. Besides, if you are losing more than winning, you shouldn't be considered a successful slacker.

Parallels to Political Elections

Procrastination is comparable to what a president does in his first two years of a four-year term. In the first two years, the president usually either vacations at Camp David every weekend, hunting pheasant, golfing, and doing nothing, or he will pass a bunch of unpopular legislation that he promised would never get passed.

Of course, the public cries out in protest and the president's popularity rating plummets. How is it that by the end of the four-year term, this type of politician usually gets re-elected? The concept is genius.

The president's strategists realize that most people don't have good long-term memories, and usually only focus on the actions and happenings of the most recent year or two. Therefore, the strategists advise the president to do whatever he damn well pleases in the first two years of the term, and then in the last half, start building that popularity rating up again. It always works out to the president's advantage, because he gets to progress his political agenda (regardless of what was promised) and still have a good chance of being re-elected. The president takes advantage of the "what have you done for me lately" syndrome that we corporate folk are all too familiar with.

The successful slacker adopts this strategy and puts it to work as a well-crafted procrastination scheme. Sometimes the successful slacker will need to actually get some work done, but usually only in the last month of a quarter or in the closing stages of a big project that is being worked on. In my situation, the first two months of a quarter are basically a vacation. I will show very low performance on the revenue side. However, in the last month, numbers come surging in and management forgets about my lack of production in the first part of the quarter.

Time Deals to Perfection

Unfortunately in sales, there is just no getting around the numbers. You have to post something up there, at least between 70 and 85 percent. Therefore, I always get **behind the eight ball** in the first two months so that I can really maximize my leisure time. Then, in the last month of the quarter, I will actually get some work done and manage to jump from about 20 percent of my number to around 80 percent. In order to do this, though, you have to be disciplined enough to put a little effort into the job. I wish it wasn't so, but it is.

Not only does this get you out from **under the microscope,** but it also impresses your co-workers and management. Just like the grand slam at the bottom of ninth, and the president improving his image in the last two years of a term, the successful slacker turns performance around at the end of the quarter so that people are flabbergasted with the improvement. Even though you only came in around 80 percent, there will be many other people who came in lower and more than likely didn't do much at the end of the quarter. Your image will be far better than theirs because the recent performance is freshest in management's mind. This is where procrastination benefits the successful slacker.

For those of you who are thinking "If I only hit 70 to 85 percent of my number, I will be put on plan or fired," you need to go back and read the chapter about finding a slacker job. In an ideal slacker job, the company is so discombobulated that hitting between 70 and 85 percent is actually an impressive feat. You are not an overachiever, yet you are not an under-performer – you are right in the middle, and that is the **sweet spot**.

The successful slacker can occasionally come in even lower than that and get away with it. In my worst quarter, I came in at 50 percent, yet nothing happened because I was usually so consistent in hitting the sweet spot that management realized I just had an "off" quarter. For once, they were right about something. Oh, I was "off" all right. I was "off" vacationing every other week. Looking back, I really pushed it too far, but damn, it was exhilarating and relaxing all at the same time.

Depending on the company, the sweet spot may be higher or lower than 70 to 85 percent. The successful slacker understands the aggregate average of the sales team, and always modifies to that number as his or her **adjusted quota**. If the average is above 85 percent, find a new job (unless it is extremely easy to hit your quota).

Lessons to Be Learned from Nebby

Nebby, like me, was one of the few employees left in the organization who worked there before the big acquisition. Nebby and I had become very close friends, due to our similar slacker work ethics and ability to close business rather quickly when motivated. We were extremely competitive, which made for some scarce moments of motivation and productivity in selling. Nebby and I were more concerned with our personal rivalry than what our quota was. He was a worthy adversary who played the political game to perfection. He was extremely conscious of his image within the team, but more importantly, Nebby was a superior procrastinator in one way, but poor in another.

Usually in sales, if a company is not bringing in the numbers they want to see, management will offer the sales team **SPIFs** which give bonus incentives to those who close business within a certain window of time. It is usually the trick to cure sagging revenues, and Nebby was cognizant of it. In order to take advantage of the system and optimize the girth of his wallet, Nebby would procrastinate to an inconceivable level, waiting for the SPIFs to emerge.

He would often have deals sitting on his desk with the paperwork signed and ready to be processed, but there was no SPIF currently being offered. He would just let it sit for a few weeks. Other times, customers would call and say they are ready to buy, but somehow he would use his powers of procrastination to relax their urgency until it benefited him more. Nebby employed the "middle of the pack" ideology in regards to quota attainment (which is discussed in the next chapter). Because he wouldn't be hitting 100 percent of his number in that particular quarter, he had to maximize commission payout. He achieved this by procrastinating on deals until the SPIFs magically appeared.

Why would you turn in a deal for no bonus when you know that in only a few weeks you may get a thousand bucks in SPIF money? Seems pretty obvious, but a lot of overachievers and other non-slackers don't have the patience or discipline to push deals out for their own benefit. Nebby would bring home more money in SPIFs at the end of the quarter than an overachiever who hit his quota would, and Nebby worked half as hard!

Despite Nebby's excellent application of procrastination in closing deals for his own financial benefit, he was less successful in applying the powers of procrastination to other areas. One habit of procrastination that really drove me nuts on a personal level was going to lunch. Nebby and I were good buddies and we would always go to the café together. We would both instant message one another to coordinate a time. We would agree to a time, say 11:15. When the time came to go, I would send a quick instant message and ask, "Are you ready?"

"Yep, let's go," he would reply. I'd sit in my office and wait because it was on the way to the café. After five minutes, no Nebby. I would IM him again.

"Hey, are you coming or what?"

"Yeah, on my way!"

Another five minutes. Nothing. After this happened a few times, I got fed up with the crap and just went to lunch by myself. Amazingly enough, he never came down. A day later, he saw me and asked, "Hey, what happened to you yesterday?"

"I went to lunch," I replied.

"Why didn't you come get me?"

This scenario happened at least once a week, and it really got irritating. Once he messaged me asking if I wanted to go eat. I told him yes and that I was coming by right away. I never came by, just to see what would happen. He never responded asking where I was. He was quite a character.

Another procrastination scenario with Nebby centered on his car. Nebby had a gorgeous house which he refurbished from **end to end** with his own hard-earned money. The house appreciated at an alarming rate due to the ludicrousness of the Silicon Valley real estate market. He had been driving the same dilapidated Nissan Maxima since college. Day after day, he would come to me and ask whether he should buy a Bimmer, Lexus, or a Benz.

Being a car buff, I told him my thoughts and offered to help. For nearly two years, this was a main point of conversation. He e-mailed and called numerous people selling their cars, and I even went on a few test drives with him, but Nebby never pulled the trigger. He would haggle, tire-kick, and just not respond to people. His procrastination was so severe that even after crashing the Nissan and destroying the hood, headlight, and bumper, he still drove it. It was not a situation where he couldn't afford a new car – his equity gain in the house could have bought him ten new cars. He was simply a hardcore procrastinator.

The poor procrastination habits he displayed on a personal level carried over into his work as well. If he had to assemble a presentation for a customer, he would always do it at the last second, and it showed. The slides in a PowerPoint deck would show the name of a different company he presented to a week earlier.

If the team got "action required" e-mails, he would not follow the recommended slacker process highlighted under "ACTION REQUIRED – Not Really." He simply would not respond to the sender at all, even if they followed up. It didn't matter how many times the manager would send him reminders to do his annual review, he wouldn't get it completed. Several people observed his behavior and the reputation started to build.

Even though he was an outstanding salesperson, the perception was that Nebby had been unresponsive in getting required tasks done. His excuse would usually be that he didn't see the e-mail, or wasn't in the office, or was busy with a customer issue, but after a while, the same excuses got threadbare. Nebby's incomplete procrastination technique compromised his entire game as a successful slacker.

He was perceived as a poor team player, he was not under the radar (because everyone was complaining about his lack of responsiveness), and both actions perpetuated a public display of the Whatever! attitude. Tigol Biddy referred to it as an "entitlement attitude," and said that pre-acquisition employees like Nebby and me suffered from it. It's funny that hypocritical comment came from her, because she displayed the identical attitude.

Nebby's behavior proves why it is essential to understand the nuances of each successful slacker habit. Yes, it is important to be a procrastinator, but do not cross the line or your entire game will be jeopardized. Nebby was terrific at procrastinating deals for his own financial benefit, but his personal procrastination and poor application in other areas of the job tarnished his image.

The reason why Nebby lasted so long was because his sales performances consistently overshadowed his lack of responsiveness and task completion. He was also a hilariously entertaining guy who everyone liked to hang with, which further justifies why successful slackers need to develop the personality attributes of Ferris Bueller. He was a hoot all right, but *damn* he was a nebby nose!

K.P.'s Notes

- Successful slackers don't procrastinate because they need the looming pressure. They do it in order to maximize their leisure time and perception within the team.
- Because management has an overwhelming "what have you done for me lately" attitude, procrastination is used to accomplish tasks when it is most critical to be productive.
- The concept of *ACTION REQUIRED – Not Really* is employed when a successful slacker is served with a task which someone deems urgent. Immediately respond to acknowledge the task, then do nothing. If the assigner follows up to check in, acknowledge again, and still do nothing. If the assigner does not follow up a third time, then it is an ACTION REQUIRED – Not Really. If they happen to follow up a third time, apologize profusely and complete the task.
- By not immediately completing the task, but being responsive, it is perceived that you are extremely busy. Therefore, the next time an assignment needs to be completed, you will not be bothered to waste time.

- In sales, procrastination can be used in order to hold deals out until the end of a quarter or year. By bringing in the whopper at the last possible minute, you are perceived as a hero who saved the day – never mind the fact you contributed little to nothing all quarter long.

- Procrastination of a successful slacker is comparable to the strategy an American president employs: Do little to nothing the first half of a term, and the second half, be more responsive and productive to improve perception in the short-term memory of American voters.

- Because successful slackers in sales usually only hit 70 to 85 percent of their number, procrastination can be used to gain significant amounts of leisure time in the first two months of a sales quarter.

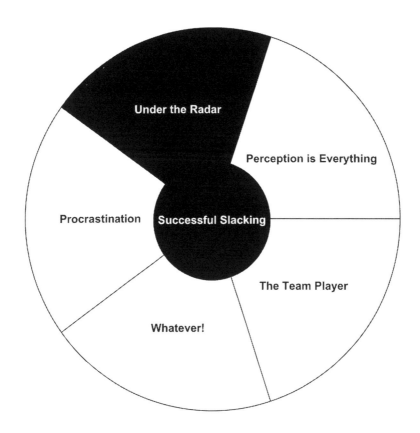

Habit Five: Under the Radar

"Accomplishing the impossible only means the boss will add it to your regular duties."

The SR-71 Blackbird was developed by the United States Air Force and first flew in 1964. With its record-setting speeds of Mach 3.3 (faster than any missile ever made), the ability to fly at 80,000 feet, and its amazingly low profile, the SR-71 is the most revered stealth aircraft in history.

The primary reason why the SR-71 could fly through the air undetected was because of its radar-absorbing and -dissipating iron ferrite material. If there was any piece of machinery that truly went "under the radar," it was without a doubt the SR-71. In fact, the SR-71 was so good that it went over, under, and even through the radar. The successful slacker does not have to hit that extreme, but you should at least be able to go under it.

Successful slackers strive to adopt the characteristics of the SR-71. Your skin has to become micro-management absorbing material so that it can dissipate the effects of such behavior. Keeping a low profile also helps the successful slacker shirk the responsibility of specific tasks and projects. The ability to move quickly is paramount, so when an opening presents itself, you can run for the door without anyone seeing. Nothing is worse than trying to leave early and getting nabbed by either your manager, or worse, your manager's manager. Being agile and quick will require some specific physical training in order to hone the ability to escape effectively.

I would recommend buying a workout video like *The Firm,* jumping jacks, running tires and stairs, suicides, and push-ups. Please consult your physical trainer for more details and advice.

"The Sidler"

Have you seen the *Seinfeld* episode where Elaine battles with a co-worker she refers to as "The Sidler"? The guy is so quiet that when he walks around, he would often stand right behind Elaine, and she wouldn't realize until she turned around and he scared the bejesus out of her. He was a terrific example of someone in stealth mode. Imagine if you had those skills. It wouldn't be fair. Even if you were in a sea of cubicles with managers all around, The Sidler could still escape. Part of his secret was that he wore sneakers, which make far less noise than dress shoes, and further enhances the importance of not having a job with a dress code.

Even though The Sidler was elusive, Elaine was successful in detracting from his stealth-like capability. She convinced him that he had bad breath, and that he should carry a box of Tic-Tacs around. We all know how much rattling those mints can make. His cover was blown. Everyone knew where The Sidler was, even if they didn't see him.

Unfortunately, I see this all too often at work. The unsuccessful slacker will have a cell phone, keys, loose change, jewelry that sounds like a wind chime, and a myriad of other items which make a ton of noise. If someone is walking around at three o'clock in the afternoon with the aforementioned items, chances are they may be trying to escape. Their attempt will be unsuccessful regardless, because even if the manager does not intercept the unsuccessful slacker, he or she will get called out the following day. Don't be the Tic-Tac guy.

Do yourself a favor and leave the loose change in the desk. Get some keys that don't make noise. Put the cell phone on mute, or better yet, turn it off altogether. Start wearing sneakers or sandals to work. Not only are they liberating and way more comfortable, but they don't make the loud clomping sound that will draw management's attention. For you folks who insist on bringing the old laptop home every night, or have your special attaché case, ditch it. Remember, the SR-71 had a low profile for a reason. Besides, what the hell are you doing at home with your work computer anyway? That is a cardinal violation of successful slacking.

Successful slackers do not carry anything into work so that when they leave, it looks like they are just going to the bathroom. If possible, don't bring a jacket inside work with you, because it is a telltale sign that you are leaving for the day. Nobody buys the "but I'm cold" excuse. Leaving the jacket at home or in the car won't work for some people, because they either live in vicinity of the Arctic Circle or they have a long trip home by foot or in a bus in the winter. Again, if the preceding scenario describes your daily commute, it is not the ideal job for a successful slacker. **Reposition your market strategy** in relation to employment opportunities.

Middle of the Pack

Successful slackers who are under the radar also adopt the "middle of the pack" ideology. Much like a running race, people only recognize and remember the folks who finish in the front or in the back of the pack. There is the winner, the loser, and the also-ran. The successful slacker is always in the also-ran category. When somebody is a winner, all of a sudden expectations come down and the management interrogation spotlight is on. They rely on you like a parasite relies on a host to help them make up for their consistent shortcomings.

When you don't deliver, they start asking questions like: What's wrong with you? Are you in it to win it? Where is your refuse-to-lose attitude? Don't you want that team lead promotion? We thought you were a superstar. The successful slacker never builds expectations beyond what the average performance is.

As was mentioned earlier, the average finish for me quarter by quarter has usually been about 70 to 85 percent, which is most times in the middle of the pack or the upper 20 percent of the team. It is so entertaining each quarter when management hands out the new quotas. They say that they're committed getting me to my goal and that the quotas are extremely attainable and fair. I usually keep a poker face, go back to my cave, and throw it in the trash with a side-splitting Whatever! laugh.

Much like high school and college, grades and attainment are usually determined by average performance. Remember the old bell curve? Based on that theory, median team quota attainment from the prior quarter is what the successful slacker shoots for. How management comes up with original attainment numbers I have no clue, but it is definitely not based off of prior quarter performances. Giving two people the same quota when one has Boston for a territory and the other has Idaho and Montana is about as fair as putting an armless man in a rowing contest. Yes, that type of malarkey does exist at my employer — the quota thing, not the armless man thing — that would be a violation of HR policy.

Keep Expectations Low

Never over-commit the delivery time of a project or the close date of a deal. It is especially important in sales. Management hates when sales reps cannot accurately forecast their deals which are coming to close. The simple solution is not to commit to anything until the deal is basically signed and returned. Buyers are usually liars, and you cannot completely trust them. If they promise you something by a certain date, and that is relayed to management, if the deal doesn't come through by the committed date, it only affects you.

People love surprises, especially good ones. There is an old saying that goes "I have no expectations, so therefore I am never disappointed." This motto usually hangs on the corkboard of a successful slacker. Lester might get irritated that I never have anything in the committed column, but he sure does love getting deals from me that I never even told him about, which just magically *happened.*

If you are prematurely committing deals, it is like being a gargantuan red dot on executive leadership's radar screen. Every week, they will talk about your quarter-million-dollar opportunity and what is happening with it. Your name will come up week after week, and before long, you will be getting phone calls from the VP, wanting updates. This is exactly why the successful slacker avoids committing to anything.

Always tell management that the opportunity is still in its early stages, even if you've been working it for six months. Don't let them pressure you into advancing commitment to the opportunity. If they ask when it might close, always give them a teaser. I usually like to say "There is an outside chance it could happen this month." The term "outside chance" really means "no chance in the deepest, darkest hell."

Keep it Vague

Another term that my co-workers always seemed to get a kick out of was **on track**. We used to have weekly **all-hands** pipeline reviews on the telephone. The director, our buddy Scrote, was based out of Boston, and we were in California. Scrote would ask each person about every individual opportunity. Some overachievers would be talking every two minutes because of their multitude of opportunities. I had about four. Each person would give a thirty-second to one-minute update on what is happening with the deal.

When it came my turn, Scrote would ask "What is happening with Axiom Enterprises?"

"That's on track," I would reply.

"On track?"

"Yep, that's on track." I'd reveal nothing more. If he pried, I'd say something like "It has a solid chance to close this month," which means that it has no way in the darkest hell, but not the deepest, darkest hell. Before long, everyone on the team was saying *on track*. It was the new corporate mocking term. "How's the two-hour lunch at 11AM today looking?"

"Oh, that's on track."

"You takin' off early today?"

"On track for that too."

The best part was when we would have a pipeline review and the close date for one of my opportunities was fast approaching, even though it had no chance to close in that particular month. When I was asked for an update, my only response was, "Oh, that's **off track**."

I swear, after I said that, there were a few of those laughs which are so explosive they sound like sneezes, but they were quickly covered up with the mute button. Scrote got pissed off and would ask for more explanation, and I would say "It isn't on track to close this month anymore." Simple, ambiguous, and vague. Just like in a court of law, the more you say, the more that can be held against you. Don't over-commit to anything and you will safely stay under the radar.

Now the critics are probably saying "You just drew more attention to yourself by being a smart-ass than actually giving Scrote what he wanted. That goes directly against your fifth habit." I will admit to guilt in this scenario. It was not becoming of a successful slacker, but nobody is perfect. Scrote was a sinister and pernicious former used-car salesman who did me wrong several times. To say I had an extreme case of angst toward him would be an understatement. I didn't want to be on his team any longer, and was going to move to a new team anyhow, so I decided to have a little bit of fun.

Extracurricular Activities

Another item that should go without saying is the successful slacker never volunteers for any extracurricular activities. The only exception to this rule is when the event somehow involves a hobby or leisure activity that you love doing.

If the goal in taking responsibility for anything extracurricular is to further your visibility, or fill up white space in your résumé, do not proceed! The prefix "extra" should be reason enough as to why the successful slacker does not participate. However, special rare exceptions can be made if the activity truly is something that you love doing outside of work. Just make sure you are not the head organizer or coordinator. All that successful under-the-radar behavior at work will become moot if you become the Cheepnis, Inc. water polo team captain.

Avoid "Reply to All" E-mails

Unless it is of the utmost importance or a perfect perception-building scenario, don't send an e-mail to the entire business unit or participate in "reply to all" e-mails. At best, it will draw unnecessary attention to you, and at worst, it will make you look like a buffoon.

One example of this was a guy by the name of Wee. I call him Wee because all day long, you could hear this guy sitting in his office saying "WEEEEEEEEEEEEE!" like a six-year-old on a roller coaster. Don't ask me why he did this, I don't know. He was a grown man and sat behind a desk with a phone and computer, like everyone else. However, the following scenario may help explain his euphoria.

One day I got an e-mail from Wee asking if I had seen a missing handle of Jack Daniel's whiskey. After reading the message in triplicate, I couldn't believe this guy sent me an e-mail about some stolen booze. However, what really made my eyes pop out of my head was the fact that Wee sent this e-mail to the entire business unit, consisting of about one hundred people with directors and managers. What would possess someone to do such a thing? At that moment, I realized the reason for all the WEEEEEEE-ing; it was the Jack Daniel's talking. It was a perplexing moment, to say the least, and further proves the reason why you should never initiate or participate in "reply to all" e-mails.

Leave the Musk at Home

One more scenario to avoid that revolves around Wee is the topic of cologne or any artificial fragrance. First of all, his cologne was so pungent that my cheeks wrinkled up into my eyeballs. Secondly, you could literally smell it from hundreds of feet away. One morning, I was walking back from the bathroom and suddenly smelled the stench of Wee, but I was still about one hundred meters from his office! It was like getting hit by an invisible night stick. After regaining my balance, I realized he had just come in the door and sat down at his desk no more than one minute earlier.

Much like Pepe Le Pew, the old French womanizing skunk from Looney Tunes, WeeWee Le Pew left that same yellow trail of funk in his wake for me to drag on. It is impossible for WeeWee Le Pew to arrive or leave the office undetected. His manager would be able to smell him trying to escape. The SR-71 was an odorless aircraft, and the successful slacker is of the same caliber. Don't be like WeeWee.

Escape Routes

Successful slackers always have a few different escape routes, depending on the situation. As illustrated in Figure 5, I had two different primary ways of getting to the "Stairway of Freedom." If I was in true SR-71 mode with no bags, jacket, or anything else, I would take the secondary escape route, past the offices of Achoo and Lester. This was a gamble, because they might see me passing by and ask me to come in their office. I also tried to avoid the stench of Wee whenever possible, but would rather hold my breath through the foggy funk than go past Achoo and Lester's offices.

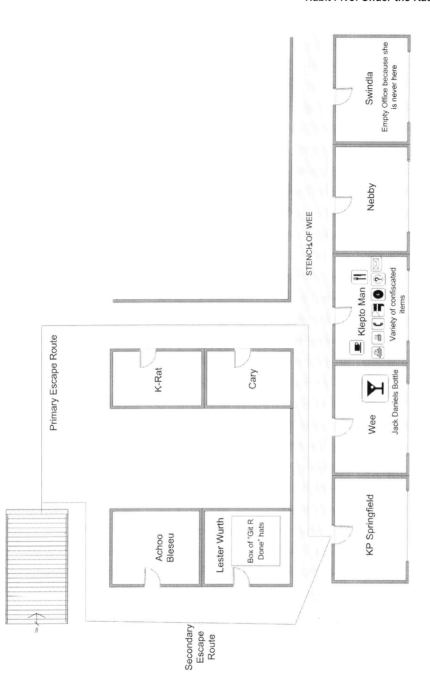

Figure 5: Escape Route Floor Plan

Lessons to Be Learned from Cary

Cary was one of the most remarkable salespeople I'd ever seen. He had such a tight rapport with customers that he ended up getting a much better job out of it. Cary came from the same direct competitor that our company had stolen every other employee from; however, he was the all-star of the company. It was like recruiting Michael Jordan away from the Chicago Bulls.

Cary was a big guy with super short hair and an uncontrollable smile. He was always happy and laughing, and he was nuts; absolutely out of his mind. He would laugh like a hyena on crack, he would run up and down the hallways like Terry Tate, office linebacker, and he would make phony phone calls all day to escort services. Imagine Chris Farley as a sales rep. Now subtract the drug addiction, the one hundred pounds of additional weight, and the fact that he is dead, and you have Cary.

He also happened to be a top-flight successful slacker. He could close more deals than any overachiever, yet still come to work when he pleased and fall asleep in his chair for most of the day. He once admitted to me that it was his territory which made him so successful, but I knew it was also his ability to sell without even having to make half of an effort. Cary was truly gifted.

One quarter, he really took advantage of the situation. The quotas were very low, and he had **sandbagged** two extremely large deals from the quarter before. By the end of the first month, he was already beyond quota. Lead after lead would come to Cary, and he would close them all. It was discouraging to others, but Cary was loving life. By the end of the quarter, Cary was a hero. Executive leadership smooched his ass till it was covered in lipstick. Cary was invited to all the management meetings, the product- and quota-planning meetings, was given a lot of leeway to talk, and was put into the "Hall of Fame." He loved every second of the attention, and was on a mission to try and get some injustices and inconsistencies within the sales team fixed. Because he was getting attention from the higher-ups, now was his chance to make his voice – and the voice of all salespeople – heard at the executive level.

After a few months he realized, like many other people have, that **driving an initiative** to change policies and practices to better the sales team was futile. In addition, because of his stellar quarter, management had suddenly put a bunch of expectations and pressure on him to perform. He was their hot prospect, so they leaned on him as expected. The leadership team turned out to be a political labyrinth in which Cary could not successfully navigate. Therefore he adopted a new **unified strategy**.

Cary started speaking the truth at meetings. He called people out when they were lying; he accused others of being incompetent; he did everything that a person would do in order to get fired because he didn't care anymore. Cary was way over the radar, not only because he super-exceeded the number, but also because he became brash and confrontational in management meetings. He stepped over the line, but he could because of how well he was selling and the fact that he was a HOFer.

Cary once mentioned to me that he made a marketing manager (who we equally despised) break into a full-on F-bomb raging fit. Cary kept verbally jabbing him in a soft spot about a product flaw until the manager started making comments like: F-this, F-that, you don't know what the F you're talking about, get out of this F-ing meeting, and so on. Cary got up in the middle of the onslaught and left the room. Almost immediately, Achoo Bleseu was in Cary's office, profusely apologizing. It was genius, because Cary then threatened to file a complaint with HR for verbal abuse and intimidation. He now had the upper hand.

Was this a good idea from a successful slacker perspective? Definitely not. He was in clear violation of habit number five: Under the Radar. However, that was Cary's choice. He made an honest effort to work hard, get his voice heard, and hopefully affect some positive change, but the politics and bureaucracy neutralized his efforts. After realizing how much worse it was to work hard and overachieve, he went back to the "middle of the pack" philosophy, stopped caring, and eventually moved across the country for a new job closer to family.

Cary was so good that he had the option to overachieve and still slack (which is impossible for most), or just slack and not hit his number. He decided to accomplish the impossible, and like the quote at the beginning of the chapter references, it set the expectation with management that he would consistently overachieve. If he were to have just slacked, finished in the middle of the pack, and had fun calling hookers at 2 in the afternoon, pretending to be a Japanese businessman looking for a good time, he may still be here today. Maybe not, but regardless, I learned a valuable lesson in successful slacking from Cary: realize the futility of the situation, and stay under the radar.

K.P.'s Notes

- Successful slackers adopt the stealthy characteristics of the SR-71 Blackbird aircraft in order to dissipate the effects of micro-management, escape from work early undetected, and avoid the responsibility of wasteful tasks.
- Never carry noisy objects like keys, cell phones or loose change, as it will detract from your ability to move about the office undetected.
- Opt for sneakers or sandals as standard work footwear, as they make far less noise than dress shoes, and are much more comfortable.
- Never carry a jacket, computer, or attaché case in and out of work, as it is a dead giveaway you are attempting to leave for the day. Besides, what the hell are you doing taking your work computer home? If you get cold easily, bring a jacket to work which remains in the office at all times.

- Successful slackers walk about the office always looking like they are just going to the bathroom. This makes for quick and easy escapes from work.

- Employ a "middle of the pack" strategy when it comes to performance. Just like in sports, everyone remembers first place and last place, but nobody remembers the "also-ran."

- When you over-perform, management relies on you like a parasite relies on a host. This brings unnecessary visibility, and keeps you from being under the radar.

- Much like grade curves in high school, attainment is determined by average group performance. By shooting for the middle, successful slackers can maintain an obscure image indefinitely.

- In sales, never commit deals to management until they are signed and returned by the customer. When deals are prematurely committed, scrutiny and attention come down from executive levels, especially if the deal is large.

- By keeping expectations low with management, they'll never be unpleasantly surprised. However, when you close a huge deal or finish a project which is unexpected, it comes as a pleasant surprise to your superiors.

- Never volunteer for extracurricular activities unless they are associated with a pastime which you love. However, if the goal is to improve your visibility within the company, refrain from taking action.

- Avoid "reply to all" e-mails, especially when it involves inquiries about a missing handle of Jack Daniel's whiskey. My co-worker Wee never recovered from that pinheaded cover-blowing incident.

- Another lesson to learn from Wee is to never wear cologne or musk which hits you in the face like a wet rag. The funk will linger for minutes, giving away your attempts to escape the office.

- Always have a primary and secondary escape route planned, in order to avoid being spotted by management.

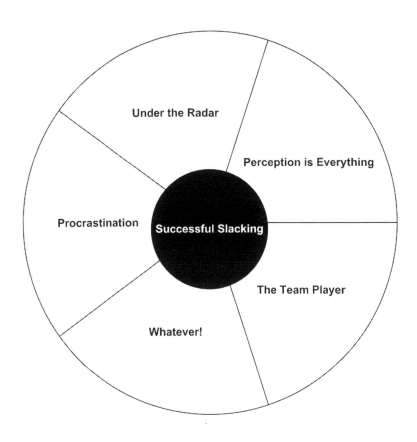

Finale

"The reward for a job well done is more work."

Now that you've read about all five habits, you may start thinking of ways these critical elements can be incorporated into personal workplace scenarios. Depending on your level of creativity, there might be new practices that you employ which could indeed result in a sixth successful slacker habit – requiring the need for a follow-up book to *The Five Habits*. Can you guess what the title would be?

During the course of *The Five Habits,* you read about some amazingly unique characters who displayed effective and not-so-effective methods in the quest to be a successful slacker. In order to get a better visualization of how they stack up in relation to successful slacking, Figure 6 summarizes performance in both their natural slacking ability and their completeness in slacking practices.

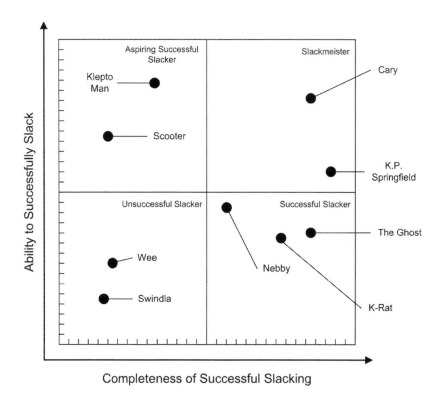

Figure 6: The Magical Quadrant for Successful Slacking

Starting from the bottom left "unsuccessful slacker" quadrant, Swindla's foul mouth and her non-team-player attitude made her the least capable at successful slacking. Wee's high profile stench, ridiculous "WEEEEE" outbursts, and hard alcohol inquiries made him second least capable. Scooter falls into the "aspiring successful slacker" quadrant because he definitely had the capability to slack, but was too honest, hard-working, and devoted to be complete in successful slacking behavior. Klepto Man, on the other hand, fits into this quadrant because he had potentially the most natural ability at successful slacking, but his poor perception really put a damper on performance.

In the "successful slacker" quadrant, although not a natural slacker, Nebby's procrastination got him to a respectable level of slacking, but his inconsistent application of it kept him from being more successful. K-Rat, who had less natural slacking capability than Nebby, was more diligent in his ability to not care yet portray himself as a devoted and hard-working employee. The Ghost, with his practically nonexistent presence, was a quality successful slacker, but his image as a potential bad apple kept him from being more successful. Yours truly falls into the "slackmeister" column because, well, I wrote the damn book! I have above-average natural slacking ability, but my complete application of all The Five Habits puts me ahead of my colleagues.

Despite my successful slacking skills, I do have some areas that need improvement, particularly my perception. Recently, my old manager Lester Wurth finally got demoted and was replaced by a guy named Muddy (not to be confused with Mud Boy). In our first one-on- one, Muddy told me that I need to be "more corporate" and that I suffer from negative perception. It was definitely a blow to my slackmeister ego, but hey, nobody is perfect.

However, the person who was by far the most talented and complete at successful slacking was my colleague Cary. His insanely likable demeanor combined with his ability to sell without even talking to customers put him on a pedestal above everyone else, including myself. It's unfortunate that he didn't come up with the idea for this book, because I am sure he might have some additional gems of wisdom to share. I will definitely be consulting his expertise for future releases and updates so you information junkies can keep abreast of all the new slacking concepts and best practices.

For You Numbers People

If you are the type of person who needs facts and numbers to be convinced, let's analyze some basic figures which should help **close the loop** on why successful slacking is a viable lifestyle. Most people work nine hours per day on average.

With some quick back-of-the-envelope math, multiply that number by five (work days in a week), then by four (weeks in a month), then by twelve (months in a year) and you get 2,160 hours. This is the number of hours an average person works in a year, not including holidays, vacation, or weekends. Now take the average amount of sleep time of eight hours per day and do the same math (we are excluding weekend days in these figures). The number comes to 1,920 hours per year spent sleeping during a work week. Now take twenty-four hours and do the math. We get a total of 5,760 hours per year of weekday time.

Let's make a few observations. First of all, most people spend more time working than they do sleeping. Second, nearly half of all weekday time (including hours in which most people are sleeping) is spent working.

Combine the 2,160-hour work figure and the 1,920 sleep figure and you get 4,080, which are the total weekday sleep and work hours. Subtract 5,760 from 4,080 and we get 1,680 hours left in the year to do what we want for leisure weekday time. That isn't much time, considering that those leisure hours are also eaten up by doing chores, tasks, and other errands which are not enjoyable and cannot be done in your sleep or during work hours.

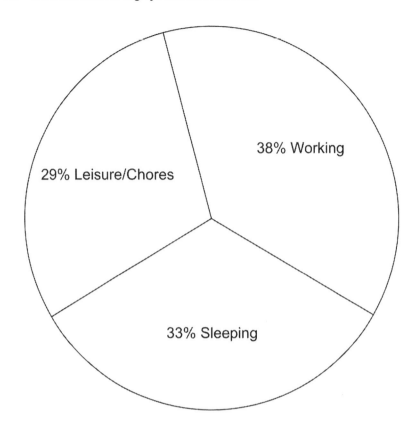

Figure 7: Back-of-the-Envelope Calculations

According to Figure 7, the statistics are alarming. **Net-net**, about 38 percent of our week (excluding weekends) is spent working, 33 percent of our time is spent sleeping, which leaves only 29 percent left over to do what we want or what we must. Are you comfortable with the fact that you spend most of your life working? Some might be okay with this because they love work. If you don't, wouldn't it be great to take a bunch of work hours and get all of your after-work chores done? How terrific would it be to schedule one of your leisure activities in the middle of a work day *and* be able to go home at the same time or even earlier and still get a healthy eight hours of sleep? All of these scenarios can be realized through the adoption of Slackism. Henry Ford may have given birth to the five-day period we now call a "workweek," but it doesn't have to be. The only obstacle in the way is your own conscience.

Americans deserve more time off than corporations give, so think of these hours you are taking as extended vacation for mental health. The mere reality that we work 5 percent more than we sleep and 10 percent more than we live makes me nauseated – and keep in mind, that is just the average! There are many poor souls like my wife who consistently pound out ten to twelve-hour days and more.

Slackism exists to help get those three percentages in a more realistic order. Leisure should be at the top of the list, then sleep (unless sleep *is* your leisure), and then of course work. Americans give new meaning to the phrase "Live to Work." If you've never visited Spain, make a trip sometime. Slackism is to Spain as modern storytelling is to Greek mythology.

The Spanish perfected the art long ago and work maybe five hours per day with three-hour "siestas" between noon and three o'clock. During these three-hour lunch breaks, they eat a huge meal and take a nap. Once they get back to work at three o'clock, you know for a fact they get very little accomplished before quitting time. I'm not lazy enough to sleep during the day, but the fact that Spaniards have a three-hour break in the middle of the workday to do what they wish underscores the priority of living life over living work in Spanish culture.

A Viable Long-term Strategy?

Although Slackism may provide successful slackers with a plethora of leisure time and stress-free work in the short term, some people have already shared feedback that Slackism is not a good long-term strategy for an employee, and that undermining the interests of a corporation will only hurt the successful slacker. Their comments are akin to what you heard in grade school when cheating on an algebra exam: "The only person you are cheating is yourself." Despite the partial truth of that ubiquitous comment, successful slackers realize when cheating is beneficial and when it a detriment. I gladly cheated on high-school algebra exams because I wasn't good at math and knew that it was a skill I would never need in the real world. To this day, that conclusion has held true.

Therefore, your individual work situation must be analyzed before adopting Slackism. If employing The Five Habits has an attractive list of benefits with no perceivable drawbacks in the long term, then why not employ it? Unfortunately, the reality in corporate workplaces is that many people achieve little remarkable success or advancement in a career which can span more than thirty-five years. Oftentimes, that achievement could have been just as easily attained by doing half the amount of work.

Not everyone has the desire or passion of becoming a senior executive within a global behemoth, or the fearless leader of a fledgling enterprise. If your goals in life include achievements not related to the workplace, then why work so hard when you can work smart, attain just as much at work, and have far more time to achieve more meaningful things in your personal life?

Alternatively, if you do not believe in the long-term merits of Slackism, consider it as a short-term strategy in order to buy more free time at work to be used for getting your desired career path or mental health back in check. It is nearly impossible to build necessary skills and interview for jobs when you're occupied with work twelve hours out of the day. Therefore, Slackism exists to open up at least six hours of your day to send résumés, hone new skills, and interview for a better life and future.

If you have already found a profession which you love but are tired of putting up with futility and the bonehead actions of executive leadership, Slackism can help you continue enjoying your craft while detaching yourself from the frustrating realities of working in a corporate environment.

Optimally, by honing The Five Habits, someone in the working world may notice your outstanding skills of perception, Whatever! attitude, team-player tactics, useful procrastination and low profile, and make you a partner in a high-billing consultant agency where those skills are used to steal wads of cash from dimwitted corporations. Remember, the corporate world did not get where it is today through the efforts of honest, trustworthy, and loyal leaders. Sometimes, in order to survive, one must fight fire with fire.

The Paradox of the Successful Slacker

After pounding you on the head incessantly with reasons why successful slacking is a viable lifestyle, some will still vehemently disagree. Executive leaders, productivity evangelists, and overachievers will probably curse *The Five Habits* and tell their friends it is ridiculous and not to waste brainpower reading it, which is totally understandable. For those people, consider this book a lesson in "how to identify a successful slacker."

After reading this book, some leaders who are productivity sticklers will possibly try to identify successful slackers and eliminate them from the ranks. However, heed caution and do not purge your team of successful slackers, because you will find that they are essential to the health of your organization. The successful slacker can be a burden and an asset all at the same time.

The demise of your entire team may come by getting rid of one solitary successful slacker. Most often, this person is the single thread that holds the tattered and beaten sweater together. People usually identify more with the slacker than they do the overachiever, and firing them can lead to bigger team morale problems. Slacker envy also plays into the equation, making a successful slacker even more popular within a group.

When faced with a particular work scenario where a decision needs to be made between taking action or doing nothing, the successful slacker always opts for the latter. Think about it from a leadership perspective; would you rather have someone who takes action and duffs the entire issue up, or have someone who does nothing and lets the problem work itself out like it often does?

Consider this scenario the next time you are contemplating the firing of a successful slacker. After reading *The Five Habits* and understanding the secrets, you may find successful slackers in your team who do not contribute much in the way of productive work. However, they're not doing anything to make you look bad as a manager, which can be far more detrimental. In fact, their superior perception qualities may actually make you look good as a leader. That is the paradox of the successful slacker — not productive enough to keep, but not detrimental enough to fire.

Protect Endangered Species

The successful slacker is a rare and iconic breed, much like a bald eagle. If you find one on the team, that person should be sheltered like an endangered species. You should feel honored to be in the presence of such a visionary. Think of this book as like the federal wildlife program which rescued the bald eagle from certain death. *The Five Habits* is here to help identify this remarkable being, protect it, and spread the gospel of Slackism. The art of successful slacking will live on, flourish, and become as essential to corporate culture as 401K plans, leather briefcases, and working lunches.

Successful slacking can happen if you believe in yourself and the cause. If the author of this book can somehow work a productivity software sales job, make the company "Hall of Fame," get positive review scores, a raise, and still get enough free time to write an entire book through successful slacking, it can happen to anyone. Ask yourself "What would I do with at least three extra hours of free time per day?"

If *The Five Habits* doesn't take off and start to change the lives of millions for the better, then well, what the hell do I care? I wrote this entire book at work! I am still getting paid, so no major skin off my back, just a massive amount of lost productivity at the expense of my employer. It will at least make a nice coffee-table book and conversation piece the next time our friends come and visit. Now are you convinced?

Slack on.

K.P.'s Notes

- According to the *Magical Quadrant of Successful Slacking,* the ranking of K.P.'s co-workers from least successful to most successful are: Swindla, Wee, Scooter, Klepto Man, Nebby, K-Rat, The Ghost, K.P., and Cary.

- Some quick **back-of-the-envelope math** calculates that people spend more than 38 percent of their workweek actually working and about 33 percent sleeping, which only leaves 29 percent for chores, leisure, and other obligations. This is a conservative average, based on a nine-hour workday. *The Five Habits* helps people get priorities realigned so that leisure and sleep come first, with work coming last.

- Some feel Slackism is not a viable long-term employment strategy. The old adage "the only person you are cheating is yourself" is often heard in relation to this topic. However, successful slackers realize when slacking is self-detrimental and when it is advantageous. Therefore, one's particular work scenario must be evaluated before adopting Slackism.

- Many career-oriented employees achieve little remarkable success over a thirty-five-year tenure, and could have achieved the same accomplishments with half the amount of work. Slackism exists to help maintain the moderate success of most employees while optimizing leisure time to enjoy life's finer things.

- Slackism can also be used as a short-term strategy in order to help an ambitious person refocus their efforts toward a more desired profession. By freeing up six hours per day, one can build the necessary skills, interview and progress themselves toward a full-time occupation they truly love doing.

- For others who love what they do but are tired of dealing with the futility and bonehead maneuvers of executive leadership, a lighter case of Slackism can be employed to reduce the emotional involvement and frustration associated with management actions.

- The successful slacker is a true paradox – not productive enough to keep, but not detrimental enough to fire. Some overachievers and productivity sticklers may even find that successful slackers can help improve their perception and image.

- Successful slackers are usually more popular than overachievers because of the Ferris Bueller effect. Therefore, firing a successful slacker may result in a morale-crushing blow to a team already downtrodden and despondent.

- As a manager, what would you rather have: an overachiever who responds to every issue and runs the risk of botching it and making you look bad, or a successful slacker who does nothing and lets the issue naturally work itself out like it most often does?

The Lingo Lexicon

-ize – an irritating and unnecessary suffix used in the corporate world to give additional motion and color to a bland term. Examples: incentivize, prioritize, revolutionize, and finalize.

Action item – a required task which needs immediate attention.

Action required – an urgent message which is usually e-mailed in order to execute an *action item*.

Across the board – universal, homogeneous.

Adjusted quota – the actual quota that one personally calculates after throwing out the quota figure given by management. Adjusted quota for the successful slacker is usually the median quota attainment for the team from the previous quarter.

All-hands meeting – a meeting that involves all members of a specific group.

All-hands-and-feet meeting – an even larger meeting involving multiple groups.

Appropriate protocol – behavior and attire that is becoming of a responsible corporate citizen.

Bad apple – see *a management problem.*

Back-of-the-envelope math – a cumbersome way of saying "quick and informal calculation."

Beachhead – a first achievement that opens the way for further developments; foothold.

Behind the eight ball – behind schedule with deadlines.

Best of breed – other related clichés are: "cream of the crop," "top of the heap," and "the shit."

Best practices – a management-approved method of the most effective and efficient way to complete a task.

BKM (Best Known Method) – see *best practices.*

Black and white – clearly evident and obvious.

Bleeding edge – a God-awful term to overemphasize the ingenuity and hyper-advanced state of a technology. Think of "leading edge" times two.

Bottom line – the crux, the point of the conversation. Also used to describe profits or revenues returned through *cost efficacy.*

Brown-noser – a universal term to describe a bootlicker, apple-polisher, or general ass-kisser in the hopes that brown-nosee will like and favor them.

Buddy system – the process by which an executive hires a friend from another company for a specific job, regardless of whether or not the candidate is qualified.

Buy in – to garner support from the *leadership team* in order to accomplish a task.

Career – a field for or pursuit of consecutive progressive achievement, especially in public, professional, or business life.

Career advancement – a meaningless term used by corporations to give validity and meaning to those sixteen-hour workdays and one-week-per-year vacations.

Catalyst – a corporate occurrence that spawns momentum in a project.

Chain of command – the formal pecking order of manager to director to VP to CXO.

Champion – a person who is favorably in charge of a project or task. Usually the champion will *drive the initiative.*

Churn and burn – process in which customers or employees are frequently acquired and lost with little regard to how it will affect business.

Circle back – to revisit a previously conversed topic.

Close the loop – to bring an official finale to a process or issue.

Commitments – a euphemistic new-wave term used to give more accountability to the previously used word "goals."

Company Kool-Aid – a metaphor which describes an overachiever or brown-noser who is seemingly hypnotized by their employer.

Core competencies – the essential skills and knowledge one possesses to be qualified for a particular role.

Corporate ladder (climbing the) – another blockheaded metaphor used to describe the path to leadership excellence.

Cost efficacy – the practice of frugal money management by leadership teams.

Cradle to grave – a ridiculously morbid way of saying "from beginning to end."

CRM and SFA (Customer Relationship Management or Sales Force Automation) – Software that is used to keep files on customers and activities. Siebel is an example of a horrible CRM.

CXO – a way of generally referring to any executive level officer (IE CEO, CFO, CIO).

CYA (cover your ass) – a defensive or offensive move taken to document and protect your innocence or disassociation with a serious issue.

Dashline (a.k.a. dotted line) – an employee whose future is undetermined. The corporate version of a sailor lost at sea. Lots of ambiguity and a perfect scenario for a slacker.

Download – the human process of receiving information, but used with a technological twist to sound more schmucky.

Drive the initiative – taking leadership action on a project.

Drop-dead point – the point at which no more work can be completed.

Ducks in a row – organized.

Eat your own dog food – using one's own company products from day to day in order to work more efficiently and effectively.

Empowered – a meaningless way of saying that an employee actually has a say in something.

End to end – see *cradle to grave*.

Executives – most times this title is self-appointed, and it depends on who you ask. Some ego-trippers will consider themselves an executive when they are only a manager. Others will consider themselves an executive simply because they work at a corporation. Most often, executives are VP level and higher.

Exit strategy – often heard in a political sense, but also used in corporate scenarios to describe the plan to terminate a project or campaign with minimal negative perception impact.

Flowchart – a useless schematic diagram used to visualize a self-explanatory process.

FUD (Fear Uncertainty Doubt) – often used in selling situations with a customer in order to make them apprehensive about a competitive solution. A corporate way of saying "shit talking."

FYI – can mean two things. FYI in a corporate sense means "for your information" and is used to start a sentence. For the successful slacker, FYI means "fuck you, idiot" and is used by itself; i.e.: "Oh yeah, FYI." "Okay? FYI what?" "Nothing, just FYI."

Game on – an often acquired term to coin the theme of a selling campaign. Much like Nike has "Just Do It," corporate sales teams will adopt terms to highlight their program.

Go to bat – action taken by a co-worker to defend another or make their voice heard.

Grade level – used in larger corporations to help in determining years of experience and setting salary guidelines.

Green pastures – a gratuitous amount of opportunity for growth and development.

GTM (go to market) – not what your wife says when you're out of cauliflower, but what executives say when they are strategizing a new approach in product release.

Hard dollar – dollar. Don't know why "hard" is in front of it. Maybe because it sounds far more certain and exact.

Hard stop – Again, the use of *hard* to emphasize. Used in meetings when someone has to leave at a specific time. "I have a hard stop at noon so we need to wrap this up."

High-level number – a corporate way of saying "guess a number between one and one million."

Housekeeping – referred to in meetings when discussing items to be completed.

In it to win it – see *game on*.

Impetus – the driving force behind any meeting, discussion, project, or initiative.

In the loop – to keep someone abreast of developments and new information.

Interdependencies – an excuse used by successful slackers in order to point the finger at other team members when *commitments* are not met.

IYF (in your face) – used after proving someone wrong or winning an argument. When used in conjunction with *FYI*, it forms a nifty little vicious and meaningful palindrome.

Keep me posted – see *in the loop*.

Key – used in the corporate world as an adjective. Examples are: key player, key initiative, key contact, key revenue target, etc.

Kickoff – An initial meeting to start a new project or cycle.

KPI (Key Performance Indicators) – also referred to as metrics. Critical data points in order to help management identify the productivity of workers. Usually related to number of phone calls or e-mails per day, or number of entries in a CRM system.

Leadership team – Most often consisting of directors, VPs, and CXOs.

Legacy – an employee of ancient status. Usually the survivor of an acquisition.

Letting you go – you're fired, get the axe, hit the bricks, pound sand, etc.

Leverage – to use a scenario or valuable information to one's advantage.

Locked and loaded – fully prepared or completed.

M&A (Mergers & Acquisitions) – the new corporate fad; when two different companies, usually in the same competitive space, decide to join in holy matrimony.

Management buffer – a process used by successful slackers to insulate themselves from pressure that is put on from executive leadership.

Management problem – a frequent occurrence in which behavior or conduct of an employee disrupts the Zen and control of a direct manager.

Mid-market – medium-sized companies that everyone wants to sell to because they have cash and are usually growing quickly.

Multitasking – to work on more than one item concurrently.

Net-Net – a perplexing term used to describe an end result. Why two nets? I don't know. Of all the corporate terms I hear, this one brings me closest to committing a homicide.

Non-recoverable draw – often heard in a sales sense and describes commission payment given to new salespeople, regardless of whether or not they sell anything. Used in the first three months of employment to entice a salesperson to start selling quickly.

Offline (Let's take this) – to discuss in private.

Off track – a sales opportunity or project which will not be completely on time or at all.

On a go-forward basis – in the future.

On task – to be *on track* with a task.

On the clock – getting paid to work.

On the same wavelength – when two or more people understand one another or have a mutual agreement on an impending scenario.

On track – see *on task*.

One-on-one – a meeting between employee and manager which is often held every week in order to keep assignments and progress updated.

OOF Message – an automated e-mail message sent in response to an incoming e-mail indicating one is out of office or on vacation.

Org chart – a diagram to help visualize the *pecking order* within a corporation.

Out-of-pocket – an irksome way of saying one is not available.

Out of the box – a unique and creative strategy or way of thinking.

Owns – To have accountability for. Used in the context "Hugh Jass *owns* that project."

Pecking order – see *chain of command* or *powers that be*.

Peel back the onion – to investigate an issue many layers below the surface.

Performance metrics – statistics to show an employee's performance. Number of phone calls per day by a sales rep is akin to the batting average of a baseball player.

Ping – a dehumanizing way of saying "contact." Originated from the action of pinging a server to see if it will respond.

PIP (Performance Improvement Plan) – a documented program for non-performing salespeople which usually states termination of employment if the person does not improve sales within a given timeframe.

Poke holes – to scrutinize.

Post mortem – document of summarized notes distributed to a team after a key all-hands meeting.

Powers that be – whoever has the ability to make a definite decision.

Prioritize – make a priority.

Push the envelope – to achieve the inconceivable.

Quorum – the minimal number of officers and members of a committee or organization, usually a majority, who must be present for valid transaction of business.

R3BC (Ringling Brothers Barnum and Bailey Circus) – acronym used to describe a company that is highly discombobulated.

Ramping up – getting acquainted with a new job through training.

Ratchet up – increase.

Refuse to lose – see *game on*.

Re-org – a corporate version of musical chairs, Twister, and Marco Polo all wrapped up into one giant activity which achieves nothing but wasted time.

Reposition your market strategy – reconsider.

Resonate – an action that someone can identify with and causes reaction.

Revenue optimization – make more money.

Revenue target – a projected financial number that will be achieved.

Revolutionizing – changing or advancing. Not only does it have an –ize suffix, but also an –ing suffix to *really* make it sound like a revolution. Corporations use this overworked term on their Web sites almost as commonly as *ROI* and *value add*.

RIF (Reduction in Force) – not to be confused with being fired. RIFs occur when companies are forced to terminate employment regardless of employee performance.

ROI (Return on Investment) – one of the most hackneyed acronyms in the corporate world. What every company uses to gauge the value of monetary or time investment.

Run it up the flagpole – to pass a message, idea, or issue up the *chain of command.*

SAA (Slacker Acronym Acquisition) – the practice of acquiring new corporate lingo and acronyms in order to more seamlessly fit into one's corporate environment.

Sandbag – people who diminish the truth for their own benefit. In a sales context, to hold a deal until it benefits the rep best; in a finance context, someone who purposefully under-commits revenue.

Satellite Campus – A secondary or tertiary location within a large company that usually displays quite a disconnect from the main headquarters.

Skill set – a list of capabilities acquired during the course of one's corporate career.

Soup to nuts – a nonsensical term used to describe a provider that can offer everything.

SPIF (Sales Performance Incentive Fund) – a bonus commission program rolled out by a sales operations team in order to motivate a sales force to sell more of a particular product or service.

Square away – to complete or finish.

SSP (Solution Specialist) – euphemistic way of saying sales rep.

Strike a chord – see *resonate.*

Sweet spot – the center, the crux, an area in which everyone shoots for.

Synergy – The interaction of two or more agents or forces so that their combined effect is greater than the sum of their individual effects; a tennis racket made back in the nineties by Prince with a cool little see-through dampener.

Take-away – lesson learned, moral of story, summarization.

Take the initiative – not to be confused with *drive the initiative.* Taking the initiative is different, in that the person doing the taking may not be the owner of the initiative. Whoever *drives the initiative* usually *owns* the process.

Talk time – the amount of time per day spent on the phone. Usually gauged by a software program and used as a *performance metric.*

Touch base – see *circle back.*

Transitioning – transition in – new employee; transition out – employee who is quitting.

Trending – progression in a certain direction that can be upward or downward.

Under the microscope – close and careful analysis. Once under the microscope, management may *poke holes* or *peel back the onion.*

Under the radar – one of The Five Habits. To keep a low profile in order to prevent unwanted attention being drawn.

Unified strategy – an approach previously agreed upon by leadership, which is carried out by the underlings.

Value add – without a doubt, the most hokey term in corporate American history. Horrifically clichéd and meaningless. Avoid it at all costs. Make up some other term.

Working remotely – to work from home or any location other than one's office.

XX,000-foot View – any number above 10,000 feet to describe the vague high-level perspective of a project or initiative. Related to *high level number*

About the Author

K.P. Springfield graduated from Indiana University-Bloomington with degrees in Journalism and Political Science. The most important realizations he derived post graduation were that he didn't want to be a politician nor a journalist. When he isn't busy evangelizing the advent of Slackism, K.P. enjoys performing music, racing bikes, writing, surfing, professional camping, 4wheeling, skiing, tennis, martial arts, horseshoes, wrenching on cars, hack web developing, honing his knowledge of useless trivia and finding angel investors for his next big business idea, Lowbucks Coffee. Contrary to what this book may have you believe, K.P. is an exceptionally focused and dedicated individual, so long as his efforts aren't futile and wasted. He's a Gemini and like long walks with his wife along the beaches of San Diego; while on the clock, of course.

Made in the USA
Lexington, KY
04 December 2010